ANDRÉ MAUROIS

TWAYNE'S WORLD AUTHORS SERIES

A Survey of the World's Literature

Sylvia E. Bowman, Indiana University

GENERAL EDITOR

FRANCE

Maxwell A. Smith, Guerry Professor of French, Emeritus
The University of Chattanooga
Visiting Professor in Modern Languages
The Florida State University

EDITOR

André Maurois

(TWAS 53)

TWAYNE'S WORLD AUTHORS SERIES (TWAS)

The purpose of TWAS is to survey the major writers —novelists, dramatists, historians, poets, philosophers, and critics—of the nations of the world. Among the national literatures covered are those of Australia, Canada, China, Eastern Europe, France, Germany, Greece, Italy, Japan, Latin America, New Zealand, Poland, Russia, Scandinavia, Spain, and the African nations, as well as Hebrew, Yiddish, and Latin Classical literature. This survey is complemented by Twayne's United States Authors Series and English Authors Series.

The intent of each volume in these series is to present a critical-analytical study of the works of the writer; to include biographical and historical material that may be necessary for understanding, appreciation, and critical appraisal of the writer; and to present all material in clear, concise English—but not to vitiate the scholarly content of the work by doing so.

Andre Maurois

By L. CLARK KEATING

University of Kentucky

Twayne Publishers, Inc. :: New York

Preface

If André Maurois can be said to belong to any one literary generation, it is that of World War I, for it was the publication of *Les Silences du colonel Bramble* in 1918 that brought him to the attention of a large and enthusiastic readership. After that date he kept his name in the public eye by a voluminous and varied production.

The life of Maurois was a full one. He had most of the honors that can come to a man of letters in France and abroad. He enjoyed the friendship of his most distinguished contemporaries, and he has had an influence on the literature of his time. He rescued biography and history from the dusty shelves of the library. In the years between the two wars he repudiated the all-too-prevalent chauvinism of his country and espoused the unpopular cause of presenting America favorably at a time when it was the fashion to seek popularity by denouncing her as a menace. He knew, as did few Frenchmen of his generation, that the world of today is one and that there is no room for parochialism. His literary life was lived in defense of idealism and a common sense morality, the first without utopianism, the second without puritanism. In spite of considerable evidence that some of the world's problems are all but impossible of solution, Maurois refused to become a pessimist. In this he was influenced by a naturally cheerful disposition and a strong constitution. He was also supported for the greater part of his adult life by a devoted and capable wife. She was not only an intelligent and loyal companion and a loving and sensible stepmother to his three children, but also, by her own wish, an indefatigable secretary and research aide. At times she sacrificed her wishes to his, helped him keep his schedule of lectures, writing, and traveling, and was in all things a tower of strength. He owed her a great deal, and of this he was not unaware.

During the course of a long career M. Maurois was reasonably fortunate in the reactions of reviewers to his books. Both at home and abroad his novels, biographies, and histories have been given careful attention in the leading periodicals. In fact, even the more crotchety and hard to please among the critics have generally found something favorable to say after reading his latest book. Few have been the dissenting voices, while the accolades have been enthusiastic in the extreme. Since this is so, it is disconcerting, especially for the foreign observer, to note that the cumulative judgments of the compilers of histories and manuals of literature are sometimes harsh, unfriendly, and downright rude. To account for this is perhaps less difficult than it might seem. After all, the histories are seldom written by the critics whose opinions of each successive book have been registered as the book appeared, but by younger men whose inevitable temper is to be iconoclastic. The latter have also been influenced by Maurois' very popularity. What more damning in the eyes of certain critics than the fact that millions of people have enjoyed his books? Are *Ariel, Byron, Disraeli* readable? Are his novels still selling well, and is his history eminently enjoyable? Then his work must perforce be of little consequence, for in the eyes of some critics popularity damns a writer as a "popularizer." Michel Droit, one of Maurois' admirers among his compatriots, has found this quotation from Voltaire which he applies with telling effect to such a point of view:

It may be thought [that] universal minds are not profound on any subject and that the word "popularization" implies "vulgarity." But this in itself is not a very profound thought. Syntheses have to be made from time to time, and writers must digest the work of the specialists for the common man. If this does not occur an unbridgeable chasm will be opened up between the technicians and the man in the street, and this would be a disaster.[1]

With this in mind, and against the opinion of those who would relegate Maurois to secondary position or even lower, the praise of Edmond Jaloux, a critic notoriously hard to please, is pleasant to encounter. He says of Maurois' work: "It is a work which will count in the literary history of our time." [2] Daniel Mornet says something similar in his *Histoire de la littérature et de la pensée contemporaines:*

You will find in (Maurois) neither dramatic power, startling picturesqueness, nor subtle and tormented psychology, but an ever balanced analysis of personalities, a lucid meditation and the wish to provide a harmonious view of reality without distortion.[3]

Maurois has had an even greater popularity in Anglo-Saxon countries than in his own. He has been, among other things, a moralist, and in France *la morale,* although taught in the schools, is suspect in sophisticated circles. It is equated there with Puritanism, a quality that the French are quite proud to do without. Throughout his career Maurois preached a strict morality, both directly and indirectly.

In 1937 Maurois' uncompromising attitude toward morality and the time-tried virtues led him to write a pamphlet entitled *La Jeunesse devant notre temps* (1937), an undevious and straightforward sermon directed toward the younger generation. In it he examines the world in which we find ourselves and urges upon youth, somewhat in the manner of a kindly uncle, the cultivation of courage, patriotism, and goodness.

Similarly he has furnished in *Ce que je crois* (1952) a collection of his random thoughts, including commentaries upon religion and a summary of his own religious attitudes. He says that he is a disbeliever in rewards and punishments after death, but declares that he is no total materialist. He believes that the civilized world is principally made bearable by the practice of such ethical conduct as is taught by all religions. As a dweller in the twentieth century, he declares himself an internationalist and a believer in democracy and has no faith in communism as an antidote for the world's ills. More recently (1959) he has furnished yet another partial summary of his philosophy of life in *Dialogues des vivants,* a work in which he gives his opinion on a variety of subjects: art, life, literary style, old age, and human relations, for example. Here, as elsewhere, Maurois so avoids the dogmatic and doctrinaire that it is hard for anyone to disagree with him, a remark which would undoubtedly have pleased him, enamored as he was of the role of mediator. But if the discussion of such homely topics is well received abroad, it is likely to irritate his countrymen. The French tradition from Rabelais to La Rochefoucauld and Voltaire prefers moralizing that is done with wit and sarcasm, and Maurois has generally denied himself the last-mentioned quality. He enjoyed satire but regarded sarcasm as an unworthy weapon for a moralist.

André Maurois was devoted to his country. He upheld the spirit of France unflaggingly, proving his patriotism, if proof were necessary, by his participation in two wars. In company with his peers he liked to think of France as a land of charm, sophistication, and civilization. During the German occupation of World War II he was a vocal and insistent defender of her cause. He regarded it as a mark of distinction that during his absence from Paris his library was singled out for burning by a special decree of the Nazi command.

And if the burning of books was a monument to Nazi immaturity
and stupidity, it was also a reminder that book-burning is the very
antithesis of everything that Maurois stood for as a man and a writer.
For him the intellect is man's supreme gift, the life of the mind,
man's greatest goal. Art, not nature, he has said, is our achievement,
for life is "a process of substitution and an orderly pattern imposed
on the phenomena of nature."[4] His own career represented an
attempt to live up to that belief.

For invaluable help in the preparation of this study on André
Maurois, grateful acknowledgment is made to the Kentucky Research
Foundation.

I am also deeply grateful to my wife, Lucille E. Keating, for assistance in preparing the bibliography and for her encouragement at
all stages of my work.

L. CLARK KEATING

University of Kentucky

Contents

ANDRÉ MAUROIS

by

L. CLARK KEATING

For more than half a century André Maurois has been a favorite of the public, and the successive publication of his biographies, histories, novels, short stories, and essays has kept his name alive in the critical journals and in the bookstores. With the writing of *Prometheus*, his biography of Balzac, which appeared in 1965, he ended his career as a biographer. Perhaps, therefore, it is time for an evaluation. The present volume attempts a comprehensive inventory.

It is not unfitting that Maurois' life and work should be discussed by an American. From the time he first met the British soldiers and officers with whom he was to fight in the first World War, up to and including his recent trip to the United States, Maurois has been a friend of the Anglo-Saxons and their interpreter in France. Similarly, when traveling or residing in Britain or in the United States he has always been a courageous interpreter of France, whether in victory, defeat, or in the sometimes more difficult days of peace. Perhaps it is too soon to hope that any study of Maurois can be in any sense definitive, but at least these pages may cast some light on his work.

Chronology

1885   Born July 26 at Elbeuf, Normandy. Named Emile Salomon Wilhelm Herzog.

1901   Year of philosophy at the Lycée of Rouen. Met Emile Chartier (Alain).

1912   Married Janine de Szymkiewicz.

1914   Mobilized. Assigned to a British army unit as a liaison officer.

1918   *Les Silences du colonel Bramble,* published under the pseudonym André Maurois.

1919–
1926   Worked in the family woolen mill at Elbeuf.

1922   First visit to the Pontigny Conference.

1923   *Ariel.*

1925   Death of his first wife. *Dialogues sur le commandement.*

1926   Resigned his position at the mill. *Bernard Quesnay.*

1927   First visit to the United States. *La Vie de Disraeli.*

1928   *Aspects de la biographie; Climats; Contact: premières impressions des Etats-Unis.*

1930   Meredith Howland Pine lecturer on French literature at Princeton University. *Byron.*

1931   Visiting professor at Harvard University. *L'Amérique inattendue. Lyautey.*

1932   *Cercle de famille.*

1933   *Edouard VII et son temps.*

1934   *L'Instinct du bonheur.*

1937   *Histoire d'Angleterre.*

1938   *Chateaubriand.*

1939   Elected to the *Académie française.* Mobilized.

1940   Demobilized. Lowell lecturer in Boston.

1940–
1944   Residence in New York. Lecturer in various colleges.

1944   Rejoined the French Army in Algiers.

1947   *Histoire des Etats-Unis; Histoire de la France.*

1949   *A la recherche de Marcel Proust.*
1952   *Lélia, ou la vie de George Sand.*
1954   *Olympio, ou la vie de Victor Hugo.*
1959   *Les trois Dumas; La vie de Sir Alexander Fleming.*
1962   *Voyage en Amérique latine; Les Roses de septembre.*
1965   *Prométhée, la vie de Balzac.*
1967   October 9. Died, after a severe illness, in hospital in Neuilly.

CHAPTER 1

Emile Herzog and André Maurois

AS several of André Maurois' biographers have noted, it is not easy to retell satisfactorily the life of an author who has himself written a charming and candid autobiography. This is especially true of Maurois, for, in addition to his memoirs, he has given us an excellent autobiographical sketch in *Portrait d'un ami qui s'appelait moi.* By so doing, he has deprived subsequent biographers of the pleasure of composing even a pithy and practical summary. At the same time, we are uniquely well informed about his life and work.

Maurois' life in France was spent in three localities: Rouen and vicinity, Paris, and Périgord. The first part of his life—his student years, his military training in a nearby garrison, his early war service —has been described by him in an early book, *Rouen.*[5] In addition to biographical data, *Rouen* offers an appreciation of the city and its role in French history. Maurois is proud to call himself a *rouennais,* for he identifies himself with the city's past and present. Most of this material was later used in his memoirs, but one reviewer so esteemed the historical part that he expressed regret that Maurois did not sufficiently describe the Rouen of today. Paris and Périgord were later conquests. The former became his home as a writer; the latter was, as it were, a legacy from his second wife.

I   A Happy Family

In his memoirs Maurois describes the family in which he was brought up; he discusses without mannerisms or apologies what it was like to be an Alsatian Jew in the country of the hardheaded Norman French. Herzog was the family name, and the boy was given the names Emile-Salomon-Wilhelm. The Germanic family name was borne proudly by a clan which which included a number of uncles of the patriarchal sort who ruled its destinies. Their life work and their greatest interest outside the family was the transplanted woolen mill established in Normandy at Elbeuf, not far from Rouen, after the loss of Alsace to the Germans in the war of 1870.

According to Maurois' account, his parents were decent, self-respecting people, quite without overweening ambition and equally without any sense of persecution about their Jewishness. Their son, our current author, relates that when he learned by accident that he was not a Christian, his father said to him soberly: "But Christianity is a noble religion and worthy of respect." This was his first introduction to religion. His second was to come when his high-school teacher, Emile Chartier, announced to his class that all religions are true, a conviction that both pleased and puzzled Emile when he heard it.

The boy was schooled at home and then enrolled in courses in the local college until he had exhausted its scholastic resources. For further schooling he entered the lycée of Rouen to which he commuted by train. In this daily excursion he was joined by a number of other young people. The students in Rouen referred to them as "the Elbeuf gang," but Maurois reports happily that, for the most part, they escaped the hazing which most outsiders had to endure. The lycée was to prove far more difficult scholastically than the local school, but Maurois tells us, not without satisfaction, that he achieved first place in most of his subjects. He won the prize even for gymnastics, a skill at which he excelled only through superhuman effort both because he had to overcome a weak back and because his main interests were in the intellectual rather than in the physical activities of the school.

Maurois' school days were obviously happy ones, but they were also something more than that, for it was in the lycée of Rouen that the future writer was to study under a master who left an indelible mark upon him: Emile Chartier, professor of philosophy and a crotchety, thorny individual and thinker who wrote essays for the newspapers under the pseudonym of "Alain." Chartier conducted his classes in an original and arresting manner, and no one has been more eloquent in his praise or more precise in his acknowledgment of his debt to him than our author. Among the latter's works are no less than three essays on Alain, covering various aspects of his teacher's philosophy and personality. The association was lifelong, and when Alain died, it was his former student who pronounced his funeral oration. The first copies of his books were for Alain, and Alain's praise was more precious to him than that of any other person.

Maurois has talked at length about Alain's teaching. He has praised his method of reading only a few books, and rereading them often. Maurois says that, like Alain, he rereads certain ones, including Balzac's *Le Lys dans la vallée* once a year. He acquired from Alain his fondness for Balzac and Stendhal, and he concludes by saying that his teacher's own works are part of his daily reading.

Critics have written with wonder as well as interest about Maurois' fondness for his old teacher. As Robert Kemp noted in a review, Alain's thought gives an impression of great effort. One digests it slowly. His former student, by way of contrast, is as light as a gazelle.[6] The extent of their friendship, given the few points of similarity between them, is therefore a remarkable case of the attraction of opposites.

For the young man from Elbeuf the philosophy course of Chartier was a revelation of a whole new world of thought and ideas, and the teacher's undogmatic, Socratic approach won him the instinctive admiration and friendship of his pupil. Nor has Maurois forgotten Alain since his demise. His continuing admiration is shown in countless ways: by reference, quotation, and anecdote in his own works. At nearly every crisis in Maurois' own life, while Chartier was still alive, he turned as much to Alain as to his own family and friends for advice and comfort. So great is Maurois' admiration for Alain that he gives him the credit for the metamorphosis of Emile Herzog, scion of a family of woolen manufacturers, into André Maurois, writer and academician. This, if true, is no small achievement.

When Emile Herzog graduated from the lycée with his baccalaureate degree, he chose to continue his studies there for another year in order to enroll once more in courses taught by his favorite teacher. But he was frustrated in this. No sooner had he made his decision than word came that Chartier had received a long overdue promotion to a post in Paris. Under the circumstances he could no longer serve as the counselor, friend and molder of the mind of Emile Herzog. At this stage in his development, however, the young man was attracted to a teaching career and, in spite of his disappointment, he decided to continue his studies through the *licence*. Writing also attracted him, but the family influence was being exerted strongly in the direction of his return to the mill. The struggle was bitter, and, oddly enough, Chartier, when consulted, agreed with the family's point of view. He feared that his pupil's precocity would lead him too soon into a literary activity for which life and experience had not yet prepared him; he felt, too, that if this happened, the young man might be sidetracked from intellectual activities for good.

Chartier's transfer meantime was a heavy blow. Maurois tells us candidly in one of his prefaces that he had always been a hero worshipper and that the loss of his hero was difficult to bear. In the lycée his reading of some of the ancient authors and of some of the French masters had influenced not only his thinking but his conduct, and he was led thereby to breaches of the morality he had learned at home. Alain's advice would have been helpful in this crisis. He had disturbed his student's conventional ideas, and now he was no longer there to help him find substitutes for them. Alain had shown him Descartes and Pascal and had led him to a new attitude toward Stendhal and Balzac. In both writers and philosophers he sought models for conduct. "My education," says our author, "began by example and continued by example. My life has been full of admiration. I try to live after the example of men whom I have respected." [7] Later in life this fondness for looking toward other men as models was to make a biographer of Chartier's pupil. During his last year at school the loss of contact with his old teacher was a huge and all but unmanageable disappointment.

When he had acquired his degree, young Herzog took Chartier's advice and returned to the mill. By so doing he perhaps escaped the role of purveyor of trashy fiction or that of undistinguished journalist, but at the time he was unhappy. He began the business at the bottom, as was the family tradition. In short order the prize-winner of the lycée heard himself characterized by one of the brutally frank workmen as a not very intelligent judge of the quality of wool. There was much to learn.

II *The War Opens New Vistas*

World War I was to change Herzog's life as it changed that of almost every Frenchman. The assignment that Maurois drew was altogether to his liking. He was ordered to liaison work with British troops in the field. The way this came about is one of those anomalies of military service everywhere. Many are the questionnaires that are filled out and replied to; few, it seems, are read. Herzog's case was different.

One day, while Maurois was still away at school, a man knocked at the door of the home in Elbeuf and asked Madame Herzog this simple question: "Does your son speak English?" On receiving an affirmative answer, the man went away. The visit was forgotten. The result, sometime later, was Emile's assignment as an army liaison interpreter. Thus he was cast in a role for which his disposition and training had fitted him, and he relished his work from first day to last. He liked the British at once, and it was his observation of the charming, the unexpected, and the paradoxical side of their character that led to his first important literary efforts. He found that nothing he had learned about the British character in the course of his English studies at school had prepared him for reality. And so, as he lived with them from day to day, the Irishman, the Englishman, and the Scot appeared ever more human and likeable. But he observed them with as much care as admiration, and all the while he was making prodigious progress in English and was expanding his meager knowledge of human nature. This was an exciting period of life which ever-present death and danger could not altogether spoil.

The end of the conflict came as something hoped and longed for, but which, from a personal point of view, had to be faced somewhat reluctantly. For the French interpreter it meant the end of years of comradeship with his British friends. Demobilization was not altogether welcome either, for it brought with it the inevitable return to the mill and an end to the philosophical conversations that he had so enjoyed. Peacetime was potentially a time of normal life—and of boredom. Little wonder that he looked back upon the war years with nostalgia as the happiest of days despite their hardship and danger. But duty beckoned, and back to the mill he went.

Unfortunately the return to the mill was only one aspect of the return to civilian life. As our author himself notes, a real conflict of interests was developing between the two sides of his nature, a conflict symbolized by his name and his pseudonym. While still serving with the British, he had asked permission to publish some sketches which dealt humorously with his reactions as a Frenchman to his British comrades. Permission was granted, but it was suggested that if his real identity were known, complications might ensue. He chose a pen name, therefore, a name quite simply constituted. His cousin André had been killed in the war, and he desired to honor him by giving life to that name. His unit was stationed near a town called "Maurois," and he took this place name for a last name. Thus the name "André Maurois" was invented. "Why after the war did you choose to keep this name and to substitute it for your own?" he has been asked. "Because," he replied, "the name at its first appearance won a considerable success. My publisher advised me to keep it since the public would henceforth recognize it." [8] Later he adopted the name legally.

The return to civilian life was more than a mere return to the mill at Elbeuf. The fate of Maurois' marriage was also at stake. With charming candor he has told us how, in the days before the war, he wooed and won a young woman of Polish descent whom he loved deeply but to whom he behaved as something of a tyrant. To complete her education before their marriage, Maurois decreed that she should go to school in England. During her stay there he played the double role of adviser and fiancé. As Maurois visited her on weekends, he essayed, in a word, the impossible task of being simultaneous tutor and lover. After their marriage he continued to manage their lives in a somewhat despotic manner and, although he did not realize it, he was sowing the seeds of discontent and rebellion. Later, while he was away at war, Maurois' wife was making new friends and acquaintances, and, despite an occasional home-leave, her husband lost contact with her. For several years their marriage drifted badly, and only his wife's early death prevented its probable break-up. The effect of his bereavement was to cause Maurois to devote more time to business than he had ever thought possible, and in a short time he was as deeply involved in the family enterprise as were his uncles and cousins. But literary contacts in Paris, which he visited frequently on business, gradually brought his mind back to his earlier ambitions. He could not forget the success achieved by his war sketches, and he kept alive the thought that he might one day become a writer after all. Inevitably, therefore, he began to reassess his importance to the family business. He soon found himself turning over his responsibilities to others in order to devote more time to reading and writing. When, at last, he decided upon a break, Maurois resigned and made writing his full-time occupation.

III *A New Life, Another War*

In time it was Maurois' good fortune to meet and to court Mlle Simone de Caillavet, a niece of Marcel Proust. The result was a marriage which stood the test of time. In due course, Maurois was to take to his heart his wife's home country of Périgord, and in all his postmarital pronouncements he includes it, along with Paris and Rouen, as a place of predilection in France.

World War II was to upset Maurois' life all over again. At the outbreak of hostilities he was mobilized and took part in the frustrating experiences of the phony war. Once again he found himself assigned to the post of liaison officer with the British army. After the defeat of 1940 he went to England to try to explain to a hostile public the unexpected and apparently inexcusable fall of France. Then, because he knew that to remain in France as a Jew and an outspoken anti-Nazi would be to invite certain and terrible death, Maurois managed to fly to the United States. To his great surprise and joy he found his wife already there. She had managed to escape France unhurt via the crowded and much-bombed roads. Her presence was a great consolation.

The years of enforced exile during the war were years of activity for Maurois as well as years of relative prosperity even though his peace of mind was shattered by the continuance of bad news from the front and the knowledge that his country lay prostrate under the heel of the Nazis. Maurois, during this period of his life, lectured in several American colleges and universities, taking as his subject various aspects of contemporary French literature. He also worked hard at the self-imposed task of apologist for the French political and military defeat. He was determined to persuade an uncomprehending and unsympathetic American public that his country had not been defeated solely because of corruption, ineptitude or cowardice, but because of the crushing superiority of German arms, a superiority that American audiences did not yet understand or would not admit. He was meanwhile drawn deeply into American life: he became a member of the Book-of-the-Month Club jury and a popular after-dinner speaker. All this he tells us in the memoirs which he wrote in America on the eve of United States' participation in the war. This concluding note was, rightly enough, one of optimism, for Maurois foresaw that her participation spelled the beginning of the end for Hitler.

IV *The Middle Years*

After World War II, Maurois' life continued along the path he had traced before the war. His year was divided into two parts: the winter in Paris; the summer at his wife's family home in Périgord. He also made frequent visits to England and the United States, sometimes alone, sometimes in the company of his wife. He also ranged over other parts of the world including Latin America, and (as is the case with nearly every literate Frenchman who travels) his wanderings furnished him a literary harvest in the form of novels, essays, and journals. Some of these were published as picture books, some as travel books, and some as thoughtful essays; and nearly all are notable in one way or another. In the time between travels, Maurois continued to enjoy both domestic tranquility and his career as novelist, essayist and biographer. He did not allow himself to become overly involved in the controversies and bitter quarrels of post-war France. He saw his task as that of mediator or benevolent neutral among opposing zealots, an attitude that brought upon his head the wrath of the combatants in all the quarrels afoot. While taking part in the deliberations of the Academy, Maurois cast his influence and his ballots in the direction of liberalism, that is, voting for younger men and against political questions as a test for membership.

Maurois undoubtedly mellowed with time. He notes in his autobiography the harshness he displayed toward his first wife, as when, for instance, he demanded of her a running account of each day's activities. He admits similarly that he sometimes gave pain to his second wife by the self-righteous rigidity of his attitudes, as, for instance, when he refused to let his children call her *maman*. Maturity changed all this and brought him a measure of tolerance, a more realistic view of his own shortcomings, and a more balanced view of the world. The Maurois of the later years was a mild man who was determined never to force his opinions upon his readers. When he wrote a book on Périgord, he did so because he wanted his readers to share his pleasure. In many a short essay and miscellaneous piece he detailed his tastes in literature and his attitude toward various aspects of life. And since he was truly a cosmopolitan, unlike his friends Mauriac and Duhamel, he was able to look at the non-French world with serenity. He thought of himself as basically French, but he noted that, like Disraeli in England, he was able to bring to France the Jewish objectivity that enabled him to see her not solely with the eyes of a patriot but in a world context as well. To prate of French superiorities everywhere he went would have been as unnatural to him as it is natural to others. For instance, while he permitted himself to praise French cooking in an introduction to his son Gerald's book, *Cooking with a French Touch*,[9] he did not by implication sneer at the cooking of other nations. This is a welcome change from the kind of chauvinism that many French writers have made an inseparable part of their writing about the non-French world. Maurois was French enough to regard many things French as superior to things non-French. Every man's patriotism and a lifetime of habit decree this much, but Maurois seldom belabored the point. Instead, he assumed the mission of telling his fellow countrymen about the unexpected delights of American cities or the joys of exploring rural England.

It seems plausible to believe that Maurois was moved in this direction not only by a natural instinct toward tolerance but by a conscious effort to imitate qualities which he admired in Disraeli. Maurois admits to having little sympathy with Zionism, although he admires the zeal of its adherents. For his part, he believed that the world would be a better and happier place if the Jews would make a contribution to the country of their residence as simple citizens thereof, without calling attention to themselves by group loyalty. The latter, he thinks, is often mistaken for an anti-national or foreign allegiance. This is why he so admired Disraeli for becoming a Church of England communicant. Because Maurois had no nostalgic interest in the ancient Jewish faith he saw little reason why the Jews of each country should not become assimilated into the dominant religion of that country. He always accepted his father's dictum that Christianity is a noble religion, although one can judge by reading the passages in his works which have to do with religious belief that he could never become either intolerant about the beliefs of others or strictly orthodox in his own.

V *The Writer's Busy World*

In the course of his lectures, essays, and books, Maurois often talked about the role of the biographer and writer of fiction; in his literary criticism he discussed his own ideals as a writer. He was passionate about certain aspects of life and could make his characters sound passionate about the same things, but he was most dispassionate about his chosen career. When he spoke about writing, Maurois preferred to restrict himself to personal attitudes and reactions; he avoided pontificating. He seldom discussed a cause with passion, exception made for his defense of France in 1940–1941. As a writer and thinker, Maurois was always prone to see both sides of a question and to realize that if he felt very deeply about something, then it was reasonable to expect that other persons must have equally cogent reasons for believing the exact opposite. This is but an added reason why he appeared to enjoy the role of cosmopolitan. He had convictions but no prejudice, passions but no hatreds.

As Maurois surveyed his long and active life, he was inclined to feel that he had had the best of three worlds. His choice of the mill after graduation was hardly a choice at all, since it was counseled both by his beloved mentor and by his family. Literature beckoned, but without conviction, as did a career in teaching; Alain had feared that his pupil would make an unsophisticated writer; and was equally afraid that he would be too narrowly confined by the classroom. The mill won out for a time, but, in his subsequent career, Maurois was able to combine writing with the profession of teaching in ideal proportions. Ever since his first public addresses in Paris and in England, it was obvious that he had gifts as a lecturer, and ever since his first teaching at Princeton, he realized that he could enjoy the classroom. But when offered a permanent post at the university, Maurois shied away because he realized that the pleasurable experience of lecturing would then be augmented by the chores of a regular faculty member. Furthermore, to accept such a post would mean turning his back on France, giving up his freedom to travel, and seriously curtailing his freedom to write.

Maurois believed, in retrospect, that his decision to remain a writer, which did not preclude teaching, was a wise one. There were numerous lectures in his subsequent experience, and when opportunities offered themselves, he generally cast himself in the role of interpreter of contemporary French literature. Then he would edit his lectures and publish them. In this way his literary production was based not only on his experiences at the mill and in the world of society, but on his experiences as a university lecturer as well.

With fame came its inevitable concomitants: requests for assistance; demands for his services on committees; invitations for ceremonial appearances. Young French writers could not resist the temptation to ask their distinguished compatriot for advice regarding their careers. They wanted to avail themselves of Maurois' kindness to write a foreword to their books. Publishers asked for the accolade of a Maurois preface to their new editions of French classics. Juries to decide on literary awards were incomplete without his name on their roster. Little wonder that he retreated annually to a country house without a telephone; still less wonder that while indulging in his fondness for travel, he sought to escape some of his less pressing and less important chores by revisiting places that he liked or by exploring territory that was new to him.

When at home, in the midst of his literary preoccupations, Maurois resisted the temptation to become involved in politics. While preaching democracy with vigor and resisting with his pen any and all attacks upon it, he was persuaded that his duty lay outside active participation. He feared, perhaps with justice, that in the politician

would be lost a man who could make a greater contribution elsewhere. He was afraid also that the role that he had chosen as a
mediator between extremes and extremists would be severely com-
promised if he were to take sides in purely parochial debates. In
matters of right and wrong he was outspoken, but he was not able
to draw a line fine enough to distinguish between the ideologies of
France's thirty-odd political parties. And on the larger issues that
have divided France since the separation of church and state, or the
events of the occupation, he preferred to be silent. He hoped to see
divisions among Frenchmen based on religious, economic and political differences finally disappear. To discuss such matters is to
bring them to everyone's attention, and he was inclined to believe
that some of the cleavages will disappear in time if they are not
deliberately kept alive by those who manipulate public opinion for
their own ends. Instead of emphasizing the opinions that divided
men, Maurois devoted his career to emphasizing those upon which
all men of goodwill can agree.

Looking back over his life and its literary shadow, Maurois was
by no means smug. As he compared his actual achievements with
what he had hoped to accomplish, he found himself a little disappointed. Still he saw in his total work some reflections not only
of his real and actual day-by-day existence, but a kind of subcon-
sciously created spiritual autobiography as well. In his work, he
says, he finds traces of all his sorrows, all his aspirations and all his
strivings. At twenty he was already certain that he wanted to be a
writer, but in retrospect he realizes that he did not yet have anything
to say. Finally fate took a hand. He notes that it was the accident
of meeting Jouvet, the actor-director, that led Giraudoux to produce
plays. In his own case the accident of being assigned to a British
unit during World War I furnished him the matter and the manner
of his first book. This book was, in essence, a confession, a witnessing
to his own reactions, and this is always a part of Maurois' writing,
a need to confide in other people, a need to say: "This is what I saw
and felt. Did you by any chance see the same thing and feel the
same way about it?" His theory is that a writer is more often than
not a man who has inner unresolved conflicts and who attempts to
resolve these conflicts by making the reader his confessor. This is
the writer's way of finding equilibrium and of integrating his personality. Some succeed in this merely by denying one side of their
character; others achieve equilibrium by some form of activity. For
Maurois the catharsis is achieved through writing. For this reason

he enjoyed talking about writing. He liked to talk about what it is that makes a writer just as he enjoyed talking about what it was that made the young Herzog of the school days happy or unhappy. The spirit of writing is thus exorcized by talking about it. In presenting the public with a collective edition of his prefaces to the work of other writers, Maurois furnished a brief discussion of writing as such, and though he had done this before, he scarcely repeats himself. Obviously it gave him pleasure to put down on paper all his thoughts about writing as a craft and profession.

Of particular interest to the student of Maurois is the collection of entries from his intermittent and unedited journal entitled *Choses nues* (1963), a title that comes out somewhat inappropriately in English as *The Bare Facts* or *The Unvarnished Truth*. In these frequently charming notes he has given us disconnected but useful pictures of his participation in the public events of his lifetime. Through his pages pass a procession of the prominent men of our time: Marshal Foch, Marshal Pétain, Lord Gort, General Eisenhower, President Roosevelt, Edouard Herriot, Raymond Poincaré, Winston Churchill, and a dozen others. We are given no stories based on hearsay but accounts of events in which Maurois took part, together with recollected conversations and quotations from the lips of those present.

Perhaps the most disquieting and disappointing of these random notes is the intimate portrait of the French Academy at work on its dictionary. Shocking or amusing, depending upon the way the reader chooses to view it, is the picture of the distinguished and deadly serious academicians as they discuss the definitions to be given words that are under consideration for inclusion in the dictionary. Apparently each member dredges up from the recesses of his memory whatever data he has concerning a given entry and presents it unrehearsed and unchecked to his confreres. They, in turn, react with similar ingenuousness. If there is reference to prior dictionaries, Maurois blunders by failing to mention it.

No less interesting and probably more important than such random passages are those in which Maurois displays his indubitable skill at creating in a few words the portraits of contemporaries, and it is a delight to see that he is equally at home with Americans, Englishmen, Russians, Germans, and his own compatriots.

In recent years old age made inroads upon Maurois' vigorous constitution, but he did not stop working. His biography of Balzac was a product of these years of elder statesmanship. He published it at the age of eighty-seven, announcing that it was to be his last major work. Meanwhile he continued to follow a schedule that would tax a far younger man, visiting the United States and England when the spirit moved him, and with the youthful spirit that still characterized him, he refused to call any of his trips a "farewell tour."

Maurois had once expressed the wish to die at his desk, but it was not to be. On October 9, 1967, after a bout of severe illness, he died in a hospital in Neuilly.

CHAPTER 2

Climates: Elbeuf and Paris

AS we have seen, it was the notion of both Maurois and his teacher
Alain that he might ultimately have a career in literature. The
philosophy professor had observed in his pupil qualities which
might one day make of him an original writer, perhaps even one
of distinction. But he exercised his influence to turn young Herzog
temporarily in the direction of the woolen mill to which his family
urgently summoned him. Alain thought that the young man needed
seasoning and a broader experience of the world, and he thought
the factory as likely a place as any other to acquire both. To Maurois
the choice, once made, seemed irrevocable, and it was with a heavy
heart that he entered the mill. As it turned out, the more than a
decade that he spent there was far from wasted. While on the job
he was able to indulge his penchant for observing human nature,
and the rigid factory hierarchy, with its gradation of ranks from
unskilled laborer to foreman and manager, afforded him a variety
of human types that he could hardly have matched elsewhere. Indeed, he never outgrew, nor wished to, the experience which the
mill gave him, and a substantial portion of his writing has had for
its base the industrial society that he came to know so well in the
mills of Elbeuf.

World War I, however, was to provide Maurois, as it did many
a comrade, the new and terrible occupation of soldier, and with it,
most unexpectedly, a time of leisure quite suitable for creative writing. It was also to provide a totally different landscape and horizon
for his observations and, within that landscape, dimensions of human
nature that continued adherence to the routine of the mill could not
possibly have provided. Maurois' assignment to the post of liaison
officer with the British army enabled him to turn his high school
English studies to his immediate profit and to the profit of his
country. The English neighbor, of whom the French had always

been skeptical, even when for long periods of time they had no reason to hate or fear him, had suddenly become the ally, the indispensable comrade in arms. Britain was the partner whose unwarlike Tommies, hating to march in step, might conceivably save France from the goose-stepping gray legions of the comic-book emperor. English speakers, all too rare in a country whose provincialism had permitted it to neglect the study of the language of the country next door, were in demand for the effective conduct of the war.

I   *Liaison with the British*

Like most young people who study a foreign language, Maurois felt a certain kinship with the people whose language he studied, and so he was prepared to enjoy his assignment. And like many another soldier in all the wars of history, he found out to his surprise that the terrible moments of tension and danger alternated with long hours of waiting and with the boring routine of the barracks and camp. Young Maurois, however, did not allow himself to be bored. He found it fascinating to observe from the vantage point of comradeship the intimate details of a Britisher's life: the way he smoked his pipe, his tastes and habits, and, above all, his quaint ways of speech. The men around him astonished him at first by sounding so frightfully like the pre-war caricatures drawn by unfriendly French critics. Then, on closer acquaintance, they surprised him by revealing that this outward seeming was not the real man at all. They soon appeared altogether human and lovable, and he began to ask himself if they might not make good copy. As the days went on, Maurois was increasingly eager to try the pen for which his labors in the mill had left little or no time. Once he had begun to write, the result grew daily until it became a fictionalized account of his wartime experiences and his day-to-day contacts with the British. For a title he chose *Les Silences du colonel Bramble* (1918). Both the author and his superiors feared possible repercussions, but publication brought instant success no less among the British than among the French.

Reading *Bramble* again today, many years after its appearance, one is still struck as on the occasion of a first reading by the undoubted charm of the episodes. Charm is a vague word to apply to a literary work, but the fact that it occurs to many readers who try to describe Maurois' book says something in itself about the mixture of sympathy, tolerance, humor and intelligence that he managed to put into his writing. Like other French writers whose daily experience in the unreal world of combat led them to self-expression as a kind of catharsis, Maurois saw the stupidity of mechanized slaughter, the cruelty of sudden death, and the agony of the wounded, but with instinctive artistry he chose to dwell on pathos rather than on tragedy, and on the human rather than on the inhuman side of the war. The choice seems to have been deliberate. Maurois' unit was often in combat, and his own life was frequently in danger, but because he was young and incurably optimistic, and because his British comrades interested him greatly, he focused his attention on them rather than on the war in which they were all engaged. In *Bramble* he created a cast of characters which he was to carry with him in the successive books of what ultimately became a series: Colonel, later General Bramble, Major Parker, Dr. O'Grady and, by way of contrast, liaison officer Aurelle who represents, at one and the same time, the author in particular and the French national in general.

The British, Aurelle decided, were a serious and noble people. Their well cultivated pose of pretending to care little for the refined aspects of civilization—poetry, music and romance—was, he thought, a false front, a pretense calculated to fool no one but themselves. Above all things they wanted to avoid the embarrassment of admitting their admiration for the unmasculine pursuit of the arts with its uninhibited appeal to the mind and the emotions.

One of the many virtues of *Bramble* is its variety. The chapters are made up of a series of narratives of daily life interspersed with vignettes of passing characters. The narrator casts a glance at the French peasants, for example, who were not above making an outrageous profit by selling meat and vegetables to their deliverers, and at the Germans who, though they never appear on the scene, are commented on and felt as a presence just beyond the periphery of the scenes that are described. The book is never bitter about the enemy or his tactics. Aurelle, the narrator, assumes the point of view of the man of sense, noting that peoples at war are, as in peace, both greedy and unselfish, religious and skeptical, kind and cruel. Above all, he did not set out to write an anti-war tract. His word pictures are far less about war than about men, and they emphasize the triviality and unimportance of national differences. The narrator felt himself caught up, along with millions around him, in a great but meaningless struggle. Protest in Maurois' day was regarded by all participants as a useless form of showing off, to be disposed of by the British in the damning phrases "bad form," or "not playing the game." Although the narrator plainly sees that this too is a pose, he seems to say that under the circumstances one pose is as good as another and that all postures are to be preferred to the arrogance of the German superman.

Judged by any standard, *Bramble* was a success. The firm of Grasset, which had only dared to risk an edition of five thousand copies for a wartime publication by an unknown author, found itself reprinting the book again and again. *Bramble* was a bestseller everywhere, and critical acclaim was as unanimous as public demand. The English translation was as enthusiastically received as the original edition, and British and American critics heaped praise on the new author.

Even before the publication and success of *Bramble*, Maurois had decided to keep on writing. Foreshadowing his tremendous literary output in the next decades, he began to branch out in several directions. His return to the characters of the first book with another about them was also a characteristic gesture, for during the remainder of a long career, once Maurois created a character that he liked he was prone to use and reuse him in successive stories. His second war book, a sequel to the first, appeared in 1922. It was called *Les Discours du docteur O'Grady*. Although its framework is the same, this volume is more philosophical than the first one because Maurois decided to use it as a vehicle for some of his favorite ideas. As a consequence, *O'Grady* has far less charm and spontaneity. Once again we meet the amusingly stuffy Colonel Bramble, proud of empire, devoted to king and country, and regarding the Germans in the same light as adversaries in a cricket match. French foibles are dwelt on a bit more insistently this time, but for strategic reasons adverse criticism of the French is generally attributed to a foreigner. Relations between the sexes come in for some discussion, foreshadowing a tendency which Maurois will intensify in his later writings. We are given to understand that the British are no less conscious than the French of the importance of sex in everyday life, but they are represented as being much more inhibited about saying so. The war, when it intrudes upon these pages, is only occasionally brutal. For the most part, the combat is seen merely as background for the conversations that are reported. The concluding chapter, in which a rabidly anti-British French officer is won over by the discovery that his British counterpart is fond of tennis, is weak and contrived.

O'Grady won a considerable popularity, but most readers and critics appeared to feel that if the author is older and wiser in his second volume, he is also less amusing. They would gladly have exchanged his newfound wisdom and sophistication for the spontaneity of the first sketches. One critic asked petulantly if Maurois intended to keep on rewriting his first book. Another, Rachilde, came up with a curious reaction. She had been almost alone in giving *Bramble* a bad review when it appeared, and so, as if to make amends or at least to go along with the majority, she said of the sketches in *O'Grady*: "They have a flavor which the armed truce that we are now enjoying cannot spoil." [10] But she found herself in the minority this time as she had been in the first instance.

No less than twenty years later, Maurois decided once again to make one of his imaginary companions of World War I the vehicle for his ideas. *Les Nouveaux discours du docteur O'Grady* (1950) was the result. As the book opens we find World War II coming to an end. O'Grady, now a renowned physician and traveler, comes to see his old friend and comrade in arms, Aurelle, who is an equally well-known French writer. The middle-aged O'Grady has not changed much. He is still the charming skeptic and the humorous seeker after truth. He talks of war as a human phenomenon and about the prospects of ending it for good. He discourses on love and jealousy and contemplates the universe. He wonders what it would be like if the cream in a cup of coffee were really a Milky Way in which as many worlds existed as are in our own galaxy. But either the flavor here is less piquant or our palate has grown tired. Maurois' book this time resembles nothing so much as an all-purpose receptacle for a heap of disparate ideas, a kind of Irish stew of his favorite notions. Indeed, he admits as much.[11] From this new O'Grady the reader learns a great deal about what Maurois is thinking, but little or nothing is added to the character of the physician. Some of the critics were kind, however. René Lalou wrote a favorable review in the *Nouvelles littéraires,* saying that here, as elsewhere, Maurois "is always in possession of all his resources." [12]

In the first volume of the collected works, Maurois included still another Bramble narrative, entitled *A la recherche de Bramble.* He had written these chapters during the phony war period of 1939–1940. In them he abandons all pretense of the light touch so admired by readers in the first two books. Because he is once again in uniform, he tries manfully to recall old times, old faces, and the days when he too was young. He admires the new generation of soldiers, "the boys," and their courageous sportsmanship and idealism, but he is aware that his age cuts him off from any real contact with them.

Here, too, didacticism raises its head, and at various points the reader is subjected to ill-disguised sermonizing. A series of ten commandments for civilians during wartime sets the tone, and there is a kind of hands-across-the-channel attitude toward the British which would have been unthinkable and unnecessary in *Bramble*. Except for a single mention of Adolf Hitler as a "strange leader," there is little talk of politics. The fact is that these sketches are slight indeed. They never recapture the insouciance and the gallantry with which Maurois infused the characters of the first book. All too frequently his remarks simply reflect the Maurois of speeches and essays, and, whatever his virtues, he is an altogether different man from the gifted amateur who wrote the original *Bramble*. As Maurois himself observes in his introduction to the first volume of the collected works, "you can't write the same book twice." [13] To which many critics have replied: "Why try?"

II *Aurelle Becomes a Novelist*

Maurois' affection for the Bramble characters is quite understandable. Their original success had delighted him, for in their reception by the public he saw the possible realization of a boyhood dream; to leave the mill for literature seemed at last an attainable goal. At the same time he felt that his success as a writer of true-to-life sketches, loosely strung together on a framework, was not a sufficient proof of his powers, and so he wanted to attempt a conventional novel.

By accident of his military assignment, Maurois found himself in 1918 in the quaint old town of Abbeville, and as he wandered around its streets, observing its old buildings with antiquarian interest, the thought struck him that he might write a novel about his surroundings. The result was *Ni Ange, ni bête* (1919). He had begun to write this novel even before *Bramble* appeared. The hero, Philippe Viniès, is a socialist in post-revolutionary France, and the story describes his courtship and marriage. Maurois also interested himself, as he was to do in all his successive novels, in the intellectual life of his hero, and to give himself scope for a conversational approach, he invented a mellow old liberal named Bernard d'Houville. In this character and in the sentiments ascribed to him are to be found whatever interest the book possesses, for candor impels one to say that this is a dull performance. The humorless radicalism of Philippe is matched by the uneventful routine of his married life, and the generally uninspired incidents of the plot.

Alain liked the book, and his good opinion, if Maurois had taken it seriously, might have done him a disservice. Few readers agreed with Alain, and the sale of seven or eight thousand copies was, after the multiple editions of *Bramble,* a clearly indicated defeat. Viewed in retrospect, and knowing as we do that this novel was composed simultaneously with *Bramble,* we are hard put to understand how the same man could have written both books. The plot of *Ni Ange, ni bête* is entirely lacking in the irony, humor and sense of character and situation that made the war sketches excellent. Our puzzlement is further increased when we learn from Maurois' introduction that his models for the hero and heroine were the poet Shelley and his first wife Harriet, whose love story he had been reading at the time. Nowhere do we find in Philippe and his wife the appealing personality and exuberance of Shelley, nor the naïve charm of Harriet. As a fatuous radical, Philippe is both unbelievable and wooden. In his own more recent estimate of the work, Maurois himself is fairly hard on it. He feels that he did not succeed in liking his hero well enough to write a good novel about him. The book's "great defect," he says, "is that it has no hero." [14] Thus *Ni Ange, ni bête* was a failure which followed on the heels of a brilliant success. No one who read this novel, and it alone, would have predicted a future for its author as a writer of fiction.

Happily for Maurois, his next prose narrative was to be a thorough vindication of his claims as a novelist, for *Bernard Quesnay,* which appeared in 1926, was a fitting cornerstone for his reputation. To write this work, he turned his mind to the years after he had left school when, before and after the war, he had served his time in the family industry. In this novel he places his fictional counterpart in a situation similar to his own. Bernard, a young intellectual newly returned home from World War I, finds himself plunged into the family woolen business in Pont-de-l'Eure, a fictional twin of the town of Elbeuf. For a while Bernard struggles against becoming emotionally involved in the business. He hopes that he can work in industry without really becoming a part of it. He retains his independence of thought and action by frequent trips to Paris where he sees old friends and maintains a mistress named Simone. Little by little his interest in his job increases as events conspire to make the problems of management more challenging. Strikes break out in the mill and claim Bernard's full attention. A world depression threatens the company's solvency, and while still inwardly resisting a total commitment to business, Bernard finds less and less time for trips to Paris and dalliance with Simone. Finally she leaves him, convinced that he does not care for her anymore. Then, in Pont-de-l'Eure, Bernard's sister-in-law Françoise, who has been neglected by her husband because he is involved in his job, turns to Bernard for affection. He succeeds in resisting this temptation, but at the same time he is relieved to learn of his brother's decision to retire from the business and move to the south of France.

The leitmotif of this excellent novel, into which Bernard's problems are woven, is the business conservatism that surrounds him on all sides. It is like a quicksand that is trying to engulf him. For young Bernard the attractions and repulsions of the business are exemplified by old Achille Quesnay, his grandfather and the family patriarch. It is he whose hatred of foreign contracts and absurdly fanatical rivalry with the factory of his neighbor, Bouchet, bids fair to destroy the business altogether. The skill of the author is displayed to good advantage, too, in his account of Bernard's gradual absorption into the pettifogging details of the mill until finally, at his grandfather's funeral, everyone notices his resemblance to the old man he has so long resisted. As they look at him standing at the grave, representing the family and the industry, they predict that with the passage of time he, too, will be a hard man of business with but a single interest in life. In strong contrast to *Ni Ange, ni bête,* the psychology of the novel is good. The family scenes are well managed and at least three of the characters are memorable: Bernard, Françoise, and Achille Quesnay. The last, without becoming a mere stereotype, is a recognizable portrait of a nineteenth-century industrialist. His portrait is among the best ever drawn by Maurois as a novelist. The business affairs which provide the background of the plot are also well managed, revealing the touch of an experienced hand since, in Maurois' case, business scenes were decidedly the product of an imagination garnished by experience. His years of enforced labor in the mill proved their worth in this novel. It was one of the author's favorites, for he also feels that his personal experience helps to make it authentic. Its chief weakness, as he himself sees it, is that because he had been intimately connected with management rather than with labor, his pictures of workers lacked something in depth. Nevertheless, *Bernard Quesnay* has remained popular through the years and deservedly so.

Two years later, in 1928, Maurois published the book that many critics consider his masterpiece, *Climats.* The task that he set himself was not an easy one: to depict a man's emotional reaction to his unhappy marriage. But he sensed an incompleteness in the first draft, and after experimenting with several solutions, he hit upon that of adding a second section to show the same man as his second wife saw him. The character that he created for this purpose, Philippe Marcenat, has something of the young Maurois in him. Like his creator, he loved not wisely but too well a beautiful but capricious girl (Odile), whose character he wished to mold by precept and example. His failure in this was conspicuous. He learned to his astonishment that his very seriousness and affection were regarded by his wife as tiresome and confining, while his protectiveness brought out all her innate rebellion and unconventionality. Finally she came to hate her environment, ran away, and died soon after, leaving Philippe hurt, bewildered, and still uncomprehending. Even his wife's death left him quite unaware that his conduct had had anything to do with her reactions and unhappiness.

Philippe's second wife's character created the same situation in reverse. Isabelle loved Philippe as he had loved Odile, that is to say, a great deal more than she was loved in return. It is from Isabelle's journal, which we read after Philippe's death, that we learn how much pain he had caused her by his nonchalance and indifference. The story is purposely complicated by the fact that Isabelle knows the story of Philippe's first marriage and is therefore well aware of her own handicap. The achievement of this novel is its psychological study of a highly disciplined yet domineering man who is confronted with the problem of living successively with two women, each of whom loves him and yet is out of tune with him in her own way. Such a study could have been dull. In Maurois' hands its emotional impact is remarkable.

The secondary characters of the novel, which are lightly but effectively sketched, are mainly unpleasant. François Crozant, who steals Odile's affections, represents a conceited and selfish playboy, as ruthless as he is attractive. Solange, the heartless flirt who tries to take Philippe away from Isabelle, is cast from the same mold. The title reflects Maurois' insistence that each person or family possesses a peculiar climate or atmosphere of its own. There is a Marcenat family climate, which is a mixture of stuffiness and rigidity; similarly, there is an Isabelle climate and a Solange climate. Parisian society is the principal backdrop of the story, but the operations of Philippe's paper factory are described in enough detail to make them real.

With *Cercle de famille* (1932) Maurois returns to Pont-de-l'Eure and the business world of the middle class. The plot revolves around the adultery of an unhappy woman named Geneviève Herpain, who has deceived an affectionate but weak husband by becoming the mistress of the local physician, Dr. Guérin. The secret of this relationship is ill kept in the small town, and Denise, the adolescent daughter of the family, is shunned at school by her hypocritical classmates who pretend to despise her because of her mother's misconduct. Denise's school life is thus made miserable, and her heartaches as a growing girl, struggling to reach maturity in such an atmosphere, are described in detail. But her cup is not yet full. Her own love affair with a schoolmate named Jacques turns out badly. He turns away from her and marries her sister. This disappointment leads to her own marriage to Edmond Holman, the son of a wealthy banker, and a man not unlike her own father. Under these circumstances it is not long before Denise allows herself to slip into the same sort of adulterous adventure that she had seen and despised in her own mother. She is not unaware of the parallel, but she continues nonetheless to lead a double life. Finally, after long years of hating her mother, she goes to visit her and finds her happily married to her former lover, Dr. Guérin. At last mother and daughter understand and forgive each other. In characteristic fashion, Maurois also introduces briefly a character from a previous novel. Philippe Marcenat's widow, Isabelle, is introduced as the wife of the successful novelist, Bernard Schmitt.

For the most part, this novel keeps the reader's attention and arouses some sympathy for its unhappy heroine. Rather incredible, however, and a flaw in the novelist's psychology, is the unexplained ease with which Denise, a childhood victim of her mother's infidelity, permits herself to inflict the same kind of torture on her own husband and children. We might at least have expected her to struggle against temptation, but she does not. The result is a flat and disappointing character, and a mediocre narrative. After all, life is, as Ramon Fernandez said in his review of the book, neither so disappointing nor so heroic as Denise dreamed that it would be.[15]

To provide a comparison between life in Paris and in the provinces, Maurois relies on lengthy conversations between his principals. The provinces, of course, come off second best, for although Maurois himself likes small towns and small town life, he cannot forbear to attack, as generations of novelists have done before him, the hypocrisy and the eternally petty preoccupations of the smaller places. By way of contrast the more intellectual Parisians talk of more general concerns, such as politics and world affairs, sometimes wittily, sometimes boringly, for despite the breadth of his views and his cosmopolitan outlook, Maurois does not always score. Indeed, the reader is led to wish sometimes that some of the conversation might be dispensed with so that he might get back to the characters.

The revolt of the younger generation is well described, and most of their conversations ring true to life. The novel still does not achieve the stature of *Bernard Quesnay,* with which it should probably be compared in atmosphere and theme, or with *Climats,* which is a far greater book. In places it is almost as dry as *Ni Ange, ni bête.*

L'Instinct du bonheur (1934) was Maurois' next novel. It was also his only truly happy narrative. The plot is relatively uncomplicated. Gaston Romilly lives contentedly with his wife Valentine and their teen-age daughter Colette on an estate in Périgord. Gaston, like Antoine, the brother of Bernard Quesnay, is a retired woolen merchant who has gone south to live in the country. He and his wife Valentine had been lovers for six years before Colette was born. Among their neighbors they are thought of as highly respectable, for their secret has been well kept. But all of a sudden the incipient love affair between Colette and the son of the neighboring Saviniac family brings painfully to mind the old story of their premarital amours. Frightened at the possible effect of a public disclosure upon their daughter's matrimonial prospects, they confide in a local dowager. She, in turn, promises to persuade the Saviniacs to overlook this blot upon the Romilly escutcheon. She succeeds in her mission by adroit references to skeletons in the Saviniac closet. But the climax is reached in the nonchalant reactions of the two young people. Gaston and Valentine await in anguish the moment when their daughter will find out the disgraceful truth. When that moment finally comes, Colette deflates her parents' ego and shocks their prudery by telling them she has known the facts of the matter since she was six years old. And when she confides in her fiancé, his smiling reply is: "Is that all?"

This is a good novel. Gaston, Valentine and Colette are well drawn. For minor characters we are reintroduced to some personages whom we have met before: the Marcenats, the Quesnays, and Denise Herpain Holman. But the interlocking directorate is presented briefly enough so that no detailed knowledge of previous novels is necessary to render the characters comprehensible. At least one critic thought that Maurois was only partly successful in his handling of the locale. Albéric Cahuet, writing in *Illustration,* accused Maurois of writing more like a tourist than a native in his description of Périgord.[16]

Terre promise, a novel dealing with the period after World War I and running into World War II, was published in 1945. Its leading character is Claire Forgeaud, the daughter of a conservative army colonel. The latter lives in retirement, nursing his bitterness. In the middle of his career he had left the army rather than obey what he regarded as anti-Catholic orders during the crisis of separation of church and state. After his resignation the colonel vegetated at Sarazac, an ancient and dilapidated estate in the south of France. He was recalled to duty during World War I but died soon after. His wife, like him, was a harsh and unimaginative person who kept her daughter under the tutorship of a man-hating English spinster. Such is the almost incredibly unpleasant family background of Maurois' heroine. In contrast to these repressed characters are Claire's cousin Sybille and her Uncle Charles, both of whom are uninhibited, straightforward people who enjoy life as Claire is unable to do. As a result of her melancholy upbringing, the latter spends a great deal of her time mooning about reading poetry and fiction, and refusing to look at real life at all. Her marriage to Albert Larraque, the leading automobile manufacturer of France, thrusts her into the arms of a wealthy but demanding husband, and she finds no happiness in marriage. When she consoles herself by falling in love with Christian Ménétrier, an obscure—and precious—poet, Larraque divorces her, but still she finds no satisfaction in her freedom. Ménétrier deserts Claire for a mistress of Larraque's, but eventually he and Claire are reconciled. During World War II, Christian, a prisoner of the Germans, tries to kill himself but fails. After his release he dies in North Africa despite Claire's tender care. At the end of the story we find Claire working as a clerk in a book store in New York and living mainly for the memory of Christian.

This plot is banal enough, and reminds one irresistibly, and to Maurois' detriment, of *Madame Bovary.* Claire is little more than a second and inferior Emma, incurably romantic and totally unprepared for life. But the chief defect of the novel is its length. To reduce it by half might improve it immeasurably. Maurois himself implies this when he says that the part of the book that he himself likes best is the description of Claire's adolescence. Much of the material is presented in the form of conversations by society people, and these interludes tend to delay the plot and make the reader impatient. Maurois, an astute observer of reader reactions, should have reminded himself that while modern readers are willing to bear with the lengthy digressions of his master Balzac, they are short-tempered about having to do so in a twentieth-century novel. And the fact that the digressive passages are well written does little to soften this judgment.

The critical reactions to this novel were mixed. Some reviewers in France, England, and the United States liked the combination of discursive passages and the story of Claire's unsuccessful search for happiness. Other did not. Certainly the work cannot be counted as one of Maurois' greatest successes.

Maurois' most recent novel is entitled *Les Roses de septembre* (1956), and some of the critics profess to find it charming. Others disagree wholeheartedly. The fact is that the telling of the story is extremely uneven. The plot is of little consequence. Guillaume Fontaine, a fatuous novelist of age sixty or thereabouts, still finds himself irresistibly attracted to pretty girls. His biography is about to be written by young Hervé Marcenat, whose relation to the Marcenats of previous novels is never explained. He is abetted in this task by the writer's jealous wife. The latter feels, and with considerable justification, that her husband owes his eminence in large part to her devotion. Now as he comes to the threshold of old age, she keeps a watchful eye upon his wayward conduct. She tolerates the mild flirtations of the aging Lothario, but serious affairs she does not tolerate, and the bulk of the novel is taken up with the latest if not the last of Fontaine's affairs. Rescue from a minor entanglement in Paris comes through the efforts of an American impresario with the improbable name of Ovid Petrasco who offers the novelist a speaking tour in Latin America. Once out of his wife's sight, Fontaine acquires as a mistress a Peruvian actress of supposedly fabulous charms named Dolores. On his return to France he promises his wife that he will end the affair, and to prove his good faith he absents himself from Paris during a visit of the actress. Then, incredible piled upon the incredible, Madame Fontaine and the actress become good friends. At this point, the story ends and we are left to hope, if not to suppose, that henceforth Fontaine will allow his roving eye to entangle him in no more serious affairs and that he will treat his wife as she deserves.

The adjective "incredible" keeps suggesting itself to describe this plot. From the first to last the situations are meretricious and forced, and the characters unreal. One wonders if the fatuousness of Fontaine is as obvious to his creator as it is to the reader. Probably not, for Maurois labors to render him sympathetic, but this he will not be for most readers. The most solid virtue of the book is the novelist's ever-present skill in capturing the spirit of places he visits. The South American locale is a reflection of his own lecture tour there during the 1950's. Especially good is his evocation of Lima, Peru. If the adventures are anything like the novelist's own, they had been better left unchronicled.

Candor requires a verdict of unsatisfactory for *Les Roses de septembre*. Among other things there hangs over the novel like a pall a heavy odor of middle-aged sensuality and the relentless pursuit of women which present-day Frenchmen must find out of date and Anglo-Saxons regard as unreal as well as repellent. Maurois freely admits that he has always assigned a large place in his work to women and love, but his painting in sympathetic tones of "un vieux satyr" is probably destined to find a well deserved oblivion.

III   *The Short Narrative*

Conventional novels account for about a half of Maurois' output as a writer of fiction. He is also a prolific writer of short stories and *nouvelles*, and many of these have considerable merit. In replying to remarks about his fiction by Jacques Suffel, an interviewer-biographer, Maurois explains at some length his reasons for liking the *conte* and the *nouvelle*. He admires the genre, he says, for the restrictions that it places upon a writer. He says that he is not drawn especially to Maupassant's kind of story but rather to the more leisurely pace of Mérimée. He does, in fact, possess two of the latter's characteristics. He enjoys and emulates his urbanity and graceful-ness of style, and he indulges from time to time in the pose of the amateur or disinterested bystander who appears to relate reluctantly a dramatic incident that he knows about. Like Mérimée, Maurois is also fond of violence and of a dramatic twist at the end.

A number of Maurois' short stories are intimately related to his longer narratives. In some cases they resemble bits and pieces of novels which could not be fitted into the finished works, and which for this reason are given an independent existence as short stories. To say this is not to criticize them adversely. Some of them are good in their own right. Others, according to Maurois, despite a similar appearance, had a quite different origin. That is to say that they were written, and their characters were created, before the long novel in which the same characters appear. In either case, we find among the short narratives a number that deal with characters al-ready well known to readers of the novels. In employing this pro-cedure, Maurois is conscious of his debt to Balzac, for he believes that the latter's insistence on the continued existence of a character, once created, is a mark of his greatness. But in the twentieth century the appearance and reappearance of characters is nothing new. Zola used the device in the late nineteenth century, and Jules Romains and others were to use it in the twentieth. Its advantage to a writer is obvious: the use of known characters relieves him of an effort of characterization in each new situation, and, as a result, the limited span of the short story can be utilized to the fullest for the development of plot. So runs the argument, but in Maurois' case few of the stories which duplicate characters from the novels add very much either to his stature as a short-story writer or to our conception of the characters. We must look elsewhere for Maurois' best short stories.

The best of Maurois' short narratives are to be found in two collections: *Dîner sous les marroniers* and *Toujours l'inattendu arrive*. Maurois included both of these in his *Oeuvres complètes,* an honor he did not bestow on all his fiction. Both of these collections adhere to a formula. The first uses the Boccaccian device of a group of persons who meet for dinner and amuse each other by telling stories. Each narrative is spectacular in some way, but the incredible plots are made credible and palatable by vivid presentation and the nonchalant yet confident air of the narrator. The first story in the first collection is characteristic as well as excellent. It tells of an old French couple of remarkable miserliness who spend the years of the German occupation in New York carefully guarding their money, which has been turned into American dollars and deposited in a trunk. Naturally they are afraid to leave the trunk alone, and so in the midst of inexhaustible wealth and spending power they are poverty-stricken and terrified.

Best known of the collection is "Thanatos Palace Hotel" which has been dramatized on both radio and television. This is an ingenious and amusing tale, and a satiric one as well. Maurois imagines that somewhere in America a place has been provided where those who are tired of life may leave it peacefully. Arriving at the hotel and determined to die, the guests gradually make each other's acquaintance until with the passage of time and the enjoyment of new friendships they announce one after another that they have changed their minds about dying. At this juncture the management carries out their original request and puts them painlessly to sleep.

The title story concerns a young American girl who marries a rich foreigner in Paris, installs her French lover as an art expert in her household, and lives in apparent happiness with a husband thirty years her senior. Carefully analyzed, the story is nothing but another trite tale of adultery, but Maurois gives it an air of reality by the natural way he introduces it. The remaining stories are principally concerned with love affairs. Least successful is one that deals with gangsters. In this story, Maurois' attempt at realism is foiled by his obvious ignorance of the kind of people he is trying to write about. The setting of the collection is excellent, and the remarks of those around the table imitate to perfection the atmosphere of a dinner party among friends.

The second volume, *Toujours l'inattendu arrive*, promises more than it is able to achieve. The stories are ironical as the title implies, but they are concerned more with character than with situation. The first story, *Le Porche corinthien*, is a charming trifle about an old husband and his wife in England who are forced by poverty to sell most of their land and to allow their old mansion to be torn down. In the course of the demolition various wallpapers come into view, and these and other long forgotten aspects of the house recall to their minds old affections and emotions. Finally before the last of the house, the Corinthian porch, disappears, the old people lay flowers upon it in memory of bygone days. It is difficult to convey in a few words the charm of this little story of less than a thousand words, for its appeal lies more in the manner of the telling than in the subject itself. Another notable story in the collection concerns the two wives of a deceased writer; his first, or divorced, wife, and his second, are both determined to write his biography. The jealousies and frustrations of the two are marvelously described, and the whole is wrapped in a delightful irony. Each woman had made the writer's life unbearable in her own way. Now after his death each seeks to aggrandize herself through his memory.

Several of Maurois' *nouvelles* are worthy of consideration. The first in point of time, called *Par la faute de M. de Balzac* (1923), is regarded by many as his masterpiece. Life, says the narrator, imitates art, and the story illustrates this aphorism. The protagonist is an ambitious and unscrupulous normal-school student. He had read Balzac's story *La Femme abandonnée*, in which a young suitor returns to a lady's parlor after being asked to leave, and by this bold act wins her love. The young *normalien* of Maurois' story is tutoring the children of a wealthy politician when he discovers that their mother is attractive to him, and so he attempts to seduce her. Remembering Balzac, he refuses to take no for an answer. To his surprise the husband is delighted with the turn of events, offers his wife a divorce, and the student finds himself with no choice but to marry her. Years later, our author pictures the hero, still young, but intellectually barren, vegetating in a Provincial lycée and married to a woman old enough to be his mother. It was "all Balzac's fault." The situation, though pat, is well managed, and deserved the praise it won from the critics.

Three other early *nouvelles*, often published with the last mentioned, gave promise of Maurois' narrative skill: *Les Souffrances du jeune Werther; Portrait d'une actrice;* and *Les Derniers jours de Pompéi*. These sketches might well be classified as capsule biographies, but though they are based on the lives of real people and on an interpretation of actual events, they deserve far better the name of fiction, a fiction based on reality but fiction all the same. The first is a fanciful recreation of the love affairs of the young Goethe. With mixed irony and tenderness Maurois tells how Goethe decided to make literary capital first out of his love affair with Charlotte, the wife of his friend Kestner, and then out of his flirtation with Maximiliane, the wife of a dull grocer. The result, as everyone knows, was the widely successful *Werther,* in which Goethe wrote himself out of love.

The second tells the story of Mrs. Siddons who had to suffer a long apprenticeship in order to become a great actress. Two love stories are also involved, those of Mrs. Siddons' two daughters, Sally and Maria. The latter was a passionate and wilful girl; the former, perfection itself. But Sally had the misfortune to take the love of her suitor, Thomas Lawrence, for granted. Maria won after all, and Sally died. The climax comes when Mrs. Siddons, every inch an actress, profits by the tears that she sheds for her daughter on stage to achieve a conscious success as a tragedienne. Maurois' irony, as he shows Mrs. Siddons standing before her mirror and reflecting on her triumph, which is due mostly to her ability to weep real tears, is as delightful as it is cruel.

The story of *Les derniers jours de Pompéi* concerns the marital woes of Bulwer-Lytton, author of the famous novel of the same name. The groom's mother had bitterly opposed her son Edward's marriage to the vivacious but disorganized Rosina, and her fears for his happiness proved well founded. Bulwer-Lytton's fatuous infidelities are also described, and we are shown his conceit as an author. In this story Maurois is less impartial than in the other two. He seems to have made up his mind to make his readers detest Bulwer-Lytton. They do so, of course, but the narrator thereby deprives himself of objectivity. Still the story is well told, and with the other two is part of a group that are among the best that Maurois wrote. Some years after their appearance, he put the three together under the collective title *Méïpe*. He explains that Méïpe is an imaginary country to which one of his children liked to withdraw, and he implies that the involvement in other people's lives that is implied by writing such tales is a kind of retirement into a Méïpe of his own.

While in the United States during World War II, Maurois was invited by the firm of Simon and Shuster to take part in a collective publishing venture. There were to be ten *Nouvelles*, each by a different author, and the title of the book was to be *The Ten Commandments*. Maurois was assigned the commandment "Thou shalt not commit adultery." Although he agreed to the proposal, he had already remarked that the idea of writing on an assigned topic was somewhat distasteful to him.[17] The *nouvelle* which he wrote is topical in character and based on an imaginary episode during the German occupation of Paris. The heroine is a young Jewish singer who, for the sake of her career, is willing to overlook the persecution of her family and her people by the Nazis for whom she performs. She is finally willing even to have herself declared illegitimate in order to continue her career which is threatened by the Nazi racial laws. Only the death of her heart-broken parents finally brings her to a realization of the enormity of her selfishness. To read this story in post-war years is to recreate admirably the emotions of those trying days, for into his writing Maurois put more indignation and protest than he generally permitted himself.

An earlier and less successful *nouvelle* was *Une Carrière* (1926), a satirical tale about a Parisian "author," who by his friendships and contacts had won a reputation without actually ever having put pen to paper. His downfall, and what he regarded as the ruination of his career, came when at the insistence of an American meddler he was finally forced to write a book. The reviews were damning, the public was furious, and the hero, Chalannes, said bitterly to his protector, Mrs. Pecks: "You have forced me to make a mess of my career."

IV *The Play of Fancy*

In addition to novels and short stories of the conventional sort Maurois has written and has obviously enjoyed writing a number of works of fantasy, a *genre* which he does not consider an easy one. The rules that he lays down for it are strict. The writing of fantastic stories requires, he says, at least a partial and temporary credibility. The tone must be sober, with no twinkle in the author's eye to give the game away. If a fantasy can maintain its air of credibility, it can be useful as well as amusing, and he cites for his French audience the satires of Dean Swift, each with its social purpose. Maurois said early in his career that he had written a little story about the future, somewhat in the vein of Huxley's *Brave New World*, but he left the tale buried among an early group of stories which he did not think worth publication. Perhaps it was just as well. Both as a young man and as a mature one, Maurois has been too gentle in spirit to be a satirist in the manner of Swift or Voltaire. For this reason, most of his satires, of which he was to write a great many, mingling social criticism with fantasy as is often done, are fairly mild in tone. Maurois is at all times too aware of the other man's problems and limitations to condemn him without pity. His fantasies and satires are meant to amuse as much if not more than to criticize. In this lies his strength, and also a weakness.

One of Maurois' earliest efforts in the direction of the satirical and fantastic tale was a short piece called *Le Chapitre suivant* (1927). This amusing little fragment, for such it purports to be, tells the story of an attack by the earth upon the moon and of the interplanetary struggle that ensues. The tone is amiable, but the attack on the political causes of war is deadly serious. Like most of his other fantastic tales, this piece can be read with pleasure by children, although, as usual, the secondary meaning is lost upon them.

Maurois wrote his first long fantasy, *Le Voyage au pays des Articoles* (1927), after a visit to the writer's conference at Pontigny. Charles Du Bos and André Gide, among others, served as models for his characters. When the story appeared, the writers present at the conference sought to identify themselves with characters in the story, and since naturally not everyone was satisfied with his portrait, there were protests. The plot of the story is simple. A footloose veteran of World War I decides to cruise around the world on his yacht. When he advertises for a crew, he is astonished to receive an application from a young woman named Anne whom, after some discussion, he signs on. Their relations throughout the voyage remain strictly that of captain and crew. Toward the end of their journey they reach a remote and unknown island where they find a topsy-turvy world. Creative writers in this land have achieved the status to which every writer aspires. As the island's recognized geniuses, they live in idleness. An inferior class of men does all the work and hopes for nothing higher than the joy of providing for the literary artists. The latter, with the passage of time, have become drones and write nothing worthy of the name. Pierre and Anne reflect sadly on all this as they leave the island.

As a fable for adults, the story's precept is clear: a writer must struggle. To possess special privileges would deprive him of the will to exercise his talent. So much, story and moral, are well and good. What is lacking is a satisfactory ending, a flaw that Maurois has permitted himself too often in his fantastic stories. Since, as we have seen, he took the *genre* seriously, it is to be wondered at that he did not realize the importance of a valid conclusion. Swift and Voltaire did better in this regard, and twentieth-century expectations are equally firm.

Le Pays des trente mille volontés (1928), a fantasy intended for his own children, is much better. In this story Maurois relies on the familiar device of taking an old saying and imagining what might happen if it were carried to a logical and ridiculous conclusion. Little Michèle is having a hard time with her lessons. In a dream reminiscent of *Alice in Wonderland* she sees herself transported to a country where children do as they please. So many children, so many wills, and she discovers that life without any sort of agreement or cooperation among individuals is most unpleasant. Even magic wands do no good if each child can use his own to undo what another has wished. This time Maurois scores without doubt. He mixes just the right touch of irony with fun and laughter, and his children enjoyed the story greatly.

Patapoufs et Filifers (1930), also intended for a youthful audience, is equally good. On a Sunday visit to Fontainebleau Woods, two children find a crack in the ground and climb down to explore it. Their adventure leads them into a new world, one in which all the fat people are pitted against all the thin ones. In the slapstick battle that ensues, there is satire on quarreling, on over-eating, on stubbornness, and on many another childhood foible.

More than a decade later, while he was in New York, Maurois wrote a story called *Nico, le petit Français changé en chien* (1945). This is a tale about a bad boy whose disposition was improved by his being changed into a dog for a day. Then he wakes up and finds out that the whole episode was nothing but a bad dream. This inconsequential tale, which is well illustrated by photographs taken by the author's son Gerald, is an undoubted reminiscence of an

English children's story which Maurois had translated in 1924 with the help of a collaborator, and which he had entitled in French *La Femme changée en renard*. It is difficult to see what Maurois intended to accomplish either by his own story or by his translation. The English yarn was not notable in the midst of a vast children's literature that fairly cries out for translation, and his later use of a similar theme is a surprising repetition.

On the whole, the fantasies for children were well received. Some of the critics thought that Maurois excelled in his short stories for children.

The readers' reactions to these fantasies for children are mixed. To some they are pure delight. Others will insist on applying to them the same criteria that they apply to adult works of fiction and using this yardstick they find the stories wanting in technique and consequently in appeal. Maurois, as is his custom, refrains from judging his work, but he comments that the writing of children's stories amused him most when his own children were small. After they grew up he felt that he lost whatever skill he had had.

Maurois wrote two additional fantasies for adults each of which runs to the approximate length of a short novel. The first was *Le Peseur d'âmes* (1931). The plot is built around the adventure of a Frenchman who goes to England to visit a friend of World War I. To his surprise he learns that his erstwhile comrade in arms is engaged in an odd sort of scientific or pseudo-scientific experiment. It seems that the nearly-mad scientist is stealing the bodies of the moribund in order to watch their souls depart from their bodies. With all the secrecy and ingenuity of a Sherlock Holmes, he covers the bodies with a glass vacuum cover and makes plans to bottle up the essence that represents the soul as it leaves the body. Soberly considered, this subject is little more than science fiction of a fairly uncomplicated sort. But Maurois' narrative keeps it going so skillfully that the reader hardly has time for clearheaded analysis of what is actually occurring. Such reader attention is the best tribute that can be paid to the author of a fantasy, for one listens to him instead of heeding one's own skepticism and common sense. Edmond Jaloux said of this story that it was "a fine story, worthy of the masters of the genre." [18] At worst it is merely an amusing but unpretentious yarn.

La Machine à lire les pensées (1937) is of special interest to Americans, for Maurois tells us that it is a product of his lectureship at Princeton. An American would have said Dartmouth, since the description of the college fits the latter more accurately, but no matter. As the title shows, the plot centers around the invention of a machine to record the usually inaudible speech that accompanies our thoughts. The results, in a faculty household, in a football game, and in the election of a new president of the college are amusing if not very profound. The chief interest for most French readers must certainly lie in the pleasant and sympathetic portrait of an American small college, for France has no exact counterpart of such an institution.

As a novel, even of the fantastic sort, *La machine à lire les pensées* suffers, as do the other fantasies, from the lame conclusion that the author has given it. When events in America have been concluded, Maurois tells us somewhat primly that Frenchmen were too sensible to let themselves be led into trouble by such an instrument and therefore the machine was not saleable in France. Another and less charitable reason for the decline of the machine and the story may be imagined, and that is a sudden apathy on the part of the writer, leading to a desire to get the novel over with. Georges Lemaître has a kinder explanation.[19] He suggests that Maurois based his conclusion on his irritation with psychoanalysis which, in the form of a fable, he was attacking as too powerful. Since the latter teaches that our unconscious ramblings are important and assumes that they may even represent far better than our conscious self what we are in our innermost being, Maurois seeks to reassure us. For him the "thoughts" which the "psychograph" registered were a kind of escapist woolgathering of no particular significance. He is telling the man who has listened to his wife's mental infidelities that they are no more important than his own, that even happily married persons occasionally stray off the reservation, if only in thought. John Charpentier takes much the same attitude in his favorable review in the *Mercure de France*.[20] For him the book is a disguised attack on psychoanalysis in the name of humanism. It would be pleasant to agree with these French critics, but repeated readings of the book, enjoyable though it is, have not succeeded in changing my own conclusion, reached after a first reading many years ago, that the book's ending is hastily contrived and represents no serious follow-through of Maurois' original intention.

V *Maurois' Stature as a Writer of Fiction*

An overall evaluation of Maurois as a writer of fiction is no easy task. He has attempted a great deal and has worked in a variety of *genres.* He himself notes somewhat ruefully that writers whose materials are as diverse as his own are the annoyance if not the despair of critics, and he thus explains the variety of his work: "When I wanted to understand a subject, I got into the habit of trying to deal with it myself. This was not intellectual conceit but a basic need."[21]

He notes that this trait has caused him to be called a "pedagogue," an appelation which does not irritate him in the least.

Faced with the dilemma of explaining Maurois' work, one can simply damn him as a man who has attempted too much and who is therefore bound to do badly from time to time; but such an attitude hardly squares with the fact that his works are printed and reprinted at home and abroad. Yet certainly some of his books are better than others. In some his gifts are wasted. In others they find memorable form.

In all his novels Maurois has consistently shown that he can dramatize a situation and create reader interest. This is true even in the poorly conceived *Ni Ange, ni bête.* The conversations that he invents to tell his stories are generally lifelike in all his fiction. They are also overabundant, which is their chief defect. Once a conversation has started, Maurois becomes so interested in what his characters are saying that he allows their exchange of opinions to outrun its usefulness. Therefore, in several of the novels the reader finds himself wishing he could dispense with further talk in order to return to working out the plot. As for the characters, Maurois has been skillful in both their creation and in their delineation. Few who have read *Climats* will forget Philippe Marcenat, Odile, or Isabelle. And a similar list of memorable personages can be drawn up for most of the novels. There are, of course, less memorable characters, but no novelist can be uniformly successful.

Justin Sauvenier, in a book that is otherwise almost a paean of praise for Maurois, has this observation to make regarding his characters: "Maurois never takes leave of decorum, and one might say that he is afraid of a violent gesture, just as a coquette is afraid of sudden movements lest she muss her dress." [22] This is a shrewd judgment, for it is quite true that most of Maurois' characters are safe and sane. When they are not, he is likely to register his disapproval of them as a moralist. We can feel, for instance, his disapproval of Odile and of Denise Herpain quite as distinctly as his approval of Bernard Quesnay and Philippe Marcenat. The moralist in him dislikes those who upset life's equilibrium even when they are persons of his own creation.

In discussing his art, Maurois remarks that *Lost Illusions* would be a suitable title for almost any great novel, since it is the shock of contact with reality and the resulting change in one's outlook that make life what it is. The same will therefore inevitably be true in the fancied account of reality that we call "fiction." Maurois' best expression of this point of view is his explanation of the relation between the real and the imaginary in the essay *Alain et le romanesque.* The individual human being, he says, is the basis of a novel. The advantage of a novel over history is that while the latter deals only with motives that are known, the novel deals with the secret and confidential. This is the novel's charm and its strength.[23]

Maurois' plots vary in quality also. His work runs the whole gamut from the intentional plotlessness of *Bramble,* where plot would have been superfluous, to the complications of *Climats,* with stages in between. Persons, it may be said, are more important to him than situations. Given an interesting character, he is confident that something will happen to him. What happens is plot, and this suffices for a novel. He seldom indulges in subplots as do many of his contemporaries. If one contrasts his fiction with the complications imagined by Jules Romains, for instance, Maurois' plots seem all but nonexistent. But such a comparison is actually meaningless. As Maurois looks at life, he does not see it as composed of complicated situations, but of complicated people. Most persons regard their lives as devoid of "intrigue" or "plot," but they get into predicaments just the same, and it is these predicaments that Maurois describes. In works of fantasy he seems to have no set attitude toward plot. If the subject at hand is best served by complications, he provides them. If a particular tale is mainly preoccupied with characters and what they stand for or satirize, he neglects plot almost entirely. In sum, Maurois cannot be regarded as a great inventor of plots like Balzac, but his inventiveness is quite equal to the task that he sets himself.

As the years have gone by, there has been much discussion regarding Maurois' breadth of vision. He admitted that he did not have and did not aspire to the breadth of a Balzac. He handicapped himself, he believed, by traveling frequently, for he was convinced that the greatest novelists have created their works out of a life of contemplation. If Proust and Mauriac have done wonders with a relatively small sphere of observation, then this is probably due to the intensity of their inner life—in a word, to their contemplation. He saw his own works as the products of his own life. His actions, his thoughts, his movements all contributed to his fiction. He repudiated as ridiculous the belief that, because of this, his works were in any sense merely disguised autobiography. Readers will find in his works, he said, episodes, persons and places from his own life. He used these materials, of course, but in the writing they underwent such thorough transformation that he himself could hardly recognize the originals. The combination is Maurois' art. In his introduction to *A la recherche de Marcel Proust*, he says that all good novels contain a considerable portion of the autobiography of their authors between their covers. He believes that *The Tempest* and *Candide* no less than Montaigne's essays reflect their authors, but he adds that very often a writer's best books are those which seem to the reader far removed from the author himself. For the case of Stendhal he cites *La Chartreuse de Parme*, which he considers a better book than the obviously autobiographical *Lucien Leuwen*. In conclusion he says: "In short, a work must be fed in mysterious fashion by its creator's passions, and the creator must not be conscious of this symbiosis and altogether obsessed with himself." [24] Above all, he has rejected the idea of producing an "annual novel." When he writes it is because he is under the stress of an emotion that practically forces him to.

What happens is something like this. A sense of unbalance, a kind of suffering inspires the novelist with a need to transpose his feelings, to give them form and thereby rid himself of them. But direct confession is satisfactory to few minds. The novelist tries to find a theme that is analogous but not identical to his inward debate. One day he finds it, and he has found the subject of his novel.[25]

This point of view is not very different from that expressed on the same subject by other novelists, and if taken seriously, which it should be, it ends the accusation of "autobiography" once and for all.

Love and sexual attraction play a large part in Maurois' novels, and the concomitants thereof are adultery, unhappiness and mental anguish. This being so, he was asked how he could be considered an idealist and a defender of women and still reduce human relations to such disagreeable and tawdry terms. His usual reply was that life is so constituted, and therefore his treatment of women and of sex is but a part of his search for absolute happiness and absolute beauty. The idealist in him would like to report that husbands are always faithful, that quarrels never arise, and that all men and women are good and true. The realist in him will not permit this, and the result is the unhappy couples and trios that he presents in his fiction. Each man and each woman seeks a partner in life who will make monogamy a nearly perfect working arrangement. Their failure to find such a person, while it grieves the idealist, gives the realist his plots. The practical Maurois had to refrain from simple solutions to problems in his novels precisely because he saw that in real life they were not solved simply. His job, as he saw it, was to set up the situation and to ask certain questions. The reply to these questions constituted the plot that the characters work out among themselves. This is to say that Maurois did not see the novel as a proposition which he must prove, and he refused to play *deus ex machina* in order to reach a solution that will please him personally, or one merely intended to attract more readers. In this he was close to his two models, Stendhal and Balzac. He was also close to them and to Alain in his declared fondness for action. In practice, however, Maurois' novels often give the impression of the exact opposite. His characters stand talking at times when every instinct of the reader demands that they do something instead. They are far too often riveted to their chairs in what must be Maurois' favorite room in a house, the drawing room.

Any conclusion as to Maurois' ultimate place as a novelist must be an ambivalent one at present. If his qualities are easy to see, so are his defects. But taking the ensemble of his output, some of his fictional writing seems destined for an honorable place in literary annals. The lofty stature of several of his contemporaries may deprive him of absolutely first rank, but his achievements are still considerable. If the inward tensions of which he speaks had been more violent, he might have been a greater novelist still. *Bramble, Bernard Quesnay,* and *Climats* have each staked out a respectable claim among readers. They are worth reading. What is more, they are fun to read.

In the United States and in Great Britain, Maurois' fiction has been well received. Much credit for this must perforce go to his translators among whom Gerard Hopkins and Hamish Miles have been outstanding. Reviews over the years have ranged from ecstatic to at least polite acceptance. Most people enjoy reading his fiction. The question of his durability will be determined by their continuing to do so.

CHAPTER 3

Ariel *and Beyond*

WITH the almost self-conscious candor that characterized him, Maurois frankly admitted that a large part of his fiction closely resembled biography. This is to say that he concentrated upon each of his heroes when writing a novel in much the same way that a biographer undertakes to relate the story of an actual life. Conversely, when engaged in writing a biography he tended to get carried away and to treat conversations and events in much the same fashion as if he were writing a novel. He became aware of this curious tendency in his writing early in his career, but, obviously, if he had not made the discovery himself, he would soon have heard about it from critics and friends. Both groups were quick to offer him advice. On the one hand he was told not to try to write novels but to confine his efforts to biography, and, on the other hand, that his real talent plainly lay in the field of fiction and that he had better let biography alone. Here is his reply:

I have found equal pleasure in historical writing and in writing novels and the two tasks, although different, have always seemed to me basically the same. The method of research is not the same. Biography or history demand immense reading and well filled and well ordered files, while the novel feeds on observation and introspection. But in each case the materials, once accumulated have to be given form, and, as best I can, the imprint of my reactions, and my nature. As Bacon said, "Art is man added to nature." This is true of biography as well as of the novel.[26]

While Maurois was still in the army, his interest in both fields really began, and it arose in such a way that the two *genres* were almost inextricably intertwined in his own mind from the very beginning. It was in Abbeville during World War I that he happened upon a biography of the poet Shelley, and he read it with fascination. As he relates in his autobiography, the reading moved him strangely, for though he was outwardly performing his duties calmly and without struggle, in actuality he was quite dissatisfied with the war-torn world and with himself at the same time. He was in an inward state of rebellion, and so he felt a curious kinship with the English poet who had reacted so violently against the world more than a century before. The practical result of this hidden conflict was for him to try to express his feelings about himself and about Shelley in a piece of fiction whose hero would represent the revolt of youth. As we have seen, the novel *Ni Ange, ni bête* was the literary result. The result for Maurois himself was a kind of catharsis and an important one because from it came the discovery that he could find in writing an outlet for his perplexities.

I Ariel: *A Tentative Biography*

From this inauspicious venture into fiction Maurois moved into biography proper and wrote *Ariel,* which turned out to be an authentic masterpiece. To say this is to fly boldly and even recklessly in the face of the critics and scholars who have had an amusing time of it pointing to its supposed bathos, its alleged inaccuracies, and the so-called false image of Shelley that emerges from its pages. By pointing to these defects, many critics feel that they have disposed of *Ariel* once and for all. Nothing is farther from the truth. The Shelley of Maurois' pages is still alive, while many of the captious critics are dead and gone. The experience of most readers is that by reading *Ariel* they come to understand and to sympathize with the Shelley that it describes in an unusual way. And all Maurois' subsequent admissions of errors of scholarship, and all the carping of those who know "the facts" have not kept many readers from thinking *Ariel* a wonderful book. It is, of course, a fair question to ask whether to call it fictionalized biography. It has been called that repeatedly. A similar epithet is romanticized biography, and a pedantic segment of the critical fraternity could not be satisfied until they had made Maurois publicly admit the shortcomings of his scholarship. To achieve this end he was invited to give a public lecture on Shelley at Columbia University, and the distinguished Shelley scholar, Professor Newman White, was present to answer and, hopefully, demolish Maurois. When the lecture took place, Maurois explained with his usual sincerity and frankness the errors he had made. He bowed before the recent discoveries of Shelley scholarship and accepted Professor White's allegations regarding Shelley's deliberate offenses against morality. White, not to be outdone, said that he, too, had been basing his conclusions on insufficient evidence and he told of still more recent discoveries that made Shelley appear even worse than formerly supposed. All this Maurois has told in detail in his introduction to *Ariel* in the complete works.[27]

The method that Maurois used to write a biography of the poet was unique. He says that he read all the books on Shelley that he could find. When he had finished, he put them aside and wrote his own. The result was, as we have seen, instant popularity for *Ariel*. Critics in England and America were unanimous in their praise, and if the first reaction is the right one, which it often is, this biography stands entrenched in an eminent position in Maurois' works. Fortunately, or perhaps unfortunately, depending on one's point of view, the controversy that grew up around it made its author a little more cautious. Being at least partly convinced that his method was in some way lacking in thoroughness he decided to make a study of the technique of biography before attempting to write another. Every subsequent biography, therefore, bears the stamp of long and arduous scholarship. Still he succeeded in keeping as a kind of trademark his deep sympathy for the subjects he writes about and the apparent ease of style and avoidance of pedantry which delighted the readers of his first biography.

II *Biography Leads to Research*

Maurois' next biographical work, *Disraeli* (1927), was still centered in England in the nineteenth century, but the resemblance between its subject and Shelley stops there. Benjamin Disraeli was in every way the antithesis of Shelley. Jacques Suffel called the English prime minister "un Shelley qui a réussi," [28] a remark that is as untrue as it is clever. Nothing is farther from the truth. Although Maurois has often written about romantics, he is far from being one. Neither was Disraeli who, as a novelist, often wrote about them. Disraeli was calculating where Shelley was unrealistic; he was shrewd, logical, and fundamentally conservative. His life as man and statesman was a study in contrasts. To tell the story of his rise to the political pinnacle of the prime ministership, his biographer had to provide the reader with a considerable fund of background information about nineteenth-century British politics, and, in so doing, he might well have lost his audience. He does not do so, however. With that particular skill that is his, Maurois presents the issues in their broad outlines without dawdling over details that would have made his study a record as dull as the archives from which its facts were drawn. As it is, he blends facts and personalities in a way that pleases instead of boring. Both man and period come alive.

Disraeli, the alien, the cynic, the dandy, the converted Jew who became the embodiment of British respectability, is seen and depicted as a man who was admirable, courageous, and tender. And he managed to remain so in the midst of the conflicting animosities and ruthless rivalries of the Victorian era which, though believing itself genteel, was frequently bitter beneath the surface. Such was Disraeli, yet with his Queen and with his wife the harsh and able parliamentarian could be charming and even romantic.

Without belaboring the point, one may fairly ask to what extent Maurois saw himself mirrored in this story of a Jew converted to Anglicanism, who wished to be as English as Gladstone and as patriotic as the Queen. One wonders if he saw a parallel in the Alsatian Emile Herzog who became the assimilated Frenchman André Maurois. On at least one occasion he hints that such is the case.

Judged by the standards of scholarship and accuracy alone, this book is stronger than *Ariel,* for the dilettante who presented a delightful but improbable Shelley has become a professional. He cites chapter and verse in the archives for his facts, and marshals an array of evidence to support his every conclusion. But he has by no means abdicated his fluid style of writing, which is still composed of narration unimpeded by overly numerous citations. The result is a workmanlike account of Disraeli and his times, as most reviewers generally agreed. Pierre Brodin called the book an "authentic masterpiece" which bears reading and rereading and which lacks the *lacunae* of a romanced biography.[29]

Maurois' second major biography, if we exclude *Ariel* as *sui generis,* is *Byron* (1930). As a choice of subject Byron had obvious advantages, not least of which was that in the course of his work on Shelley the biographer had come to know a great deal about Byron. We may also assume that for an educated Frenchman such as Maurois, who had studied and admired the French Romantic movement and its heroes while in school, it was not difficult to understand the frenzies, the occasional satanism and the lack of restraint of the English Romantics. Being a Frenchman and a foreigner even had advantages. The English have never really accepted Romanticism as anything more than a kind of temporary and curious aberration, while in France the Romantics are still the object of adulation. Maurois was therefore prepared for the kind of man he found in Lord Byron. But he was not and could not be totally prepared. In Byron he found, as have all the poet's biographers, a man determinedly and ruthlessly bent on being what the Shelleys and Mussets of the time were merely playing at being: a truly evil and anti-social individual. This fact made an understanding of his character and the attempt to understand his motives extremely difficult. In order to do so and to feel some sympathy for him, Maurois formulated an unproved but ingenious theory: that Byron, for all his viciousness, was a Calvinist at heart, and that in the midst of his deliberate evildoing he was delighted and appalled at one and the same time by the conviction that his conduct was altogether wicked, that it was punishable, and would be punished by eternal hell fire. The biography becomes, therefore, among other things an attempt to demonstrate the truth of this point of view.

Byron is long. Its pages spare no details concerning its subject's perfidy, malice, cruelty, and lechery, or his skill as a poet. The criticism directed at *Ariel,* that it hardly took the poet's works into account, cannot be made here. We are informed about the poetry at every step, but, even so, Byron's personality and character were such that his poetic works are all but swallowed up in the account of his actions. Like Faust, to whom he has often been compared, he was a doomed spectator at his self-induced process of destruction. We are told nonetheless what poetry he wrote, where and under what circumstances, and we are given excerpts from the best of it. But such is the fascination of the life which unfolds that the reader almost comes to regard the poetic passages in the text as a kind of intrusion, and details of Byron's literary career as a kind of digression.

It is not Byron's actions alone that make him memorable. His galaxy of friends and associates, queer as some of them are—the Hobhouses, and Scrope Davies, his strange collection of boxers, gondoliers, monkeys, and dogs that accompanied him everywhere—make him an unforgettable if fantastic figure. And these secondary figures in his life, mistresses and confidants, odd men and animals, are all brought to life by our biographer with as much skill as is expended on his hero. Above all we see Byron's horrible self-consciousness that made him desire death as a way of finding peace, that made him seek an ordered life by achieving the absence of life, wanting the good sometimes but because, as he said, "his hands led to wickedness," being unable to reach it. At the end of the biography, in spite of feelings of irritation toward Byron that alternate with downright animosity, the reader is finally able to say, "R.I.P."

To have induced this much sympathy for Byron is not the least of Maurois' achievements.

The most serious adverse criticism is that here, for the first time, Maurois' desire to satisfy his aspirations as a professional biographer has led him into overindulgence in quotations. By their use he asserts that the story, incredible as it sounds, is true, and that Byron's own words are here to prove it. As one can tell from the appended bibliographies, *Disraeli* was equally well documented, but the insertion of quotations from the subject's papers was not allowed to intrude so frequently upon the narrative. In *Byron* and subsequent biographies Maurois will not shake off this habit of an excessive use of citations, and if he thereby proves beyond cavil the depth of his scholarship, he detracts at the same time from the easy flow of the narrative which was one of the notable charms of *Ariel*.

The publication of *Byron* was considered by many a major literary event. It was also an occasion for attacks upon Maurois' integrity. He was accused of plagiarism in four of his books: *Ariel, Disraeli, Byron,* and *Voyage au pays des Articoles.* According to his detractors, Maurois had stolen most of his biographical material and had filched the plot of his fantasy from an already published story. Edmond Gosse, the British man of letters, who was cited by the attackers as a witness for the prosecution, came to Maurois' defense and said that he could find no grounds for the accusations. After all, he observed, in writing the story of a man's life, all biographers are bound to refer to the same facts. While the battle raged, a minor critic named Georges Batault attacked Maurois in the *Mercure de France,* calling him an unscrupulous man whose chief thought was to make money through the astute uses of advertising. After a while the noise died down, but it was doubtless this episode that caused Maurois to remark in his memoirs that in mid-career he had been suddenly astonished to learn that he had enemies. He also adds that the strangest thing about their enmity was that he was not acquainted with his accusers. They were, to a man, persons he did not know. In retrospect it may be said that nobody else knows them either.

III *Other Biographies of the Thirties*

About a year after the appearance of *Byron,* in 1931, Maurois ploughed new ground by turning from nineteenth-century England to France and Russia. As the subject of a lecture series for the Société des Conférences, he chose the life and works of Ivan Turgenev, and he later published his lectures in book form. He is careful not to call this work a biography. His word for it is biographical sketch. In this study he leans heavily and without apology on published works. Sketch or biography, this short book is different from his previous ones. Whereas he had been accustomed to focus his attention primarily upon the man behind the works, in *Tourgueniev* he concentrates principally upon his subject's writings. It is true that we come to know the man, the weak-willed, soft-voiced giant who spent most of his life in Paris, and our attention is drawn to the Russian land from which Turgenev sprang and to the family from which he escaped. His chief preoccupation as a writer was the non-acceptance of his works in his own country, a failure that cast a pall of gloom over his life.

The story, though brief, is exceedingly well told. Maurois evokes the life of Russia during the nineteenth century. He introduces the intellectuals, Pan-Slavists, pro-Europeans, and nihilists, and behind them the masses of Russian peasants on farms. Turgenev's mother, for instance, owned many villages, and with them more than 5,000 people. We are told about the quarrel between Turgenev and Tolstoy, and we wonder at the brutal frankness which the two writers used with each other. The picture is memorable and no less delightful because it is short and evocative rather than heavily factual. Maurois' claims for this biographical-critical sketch are modest. He said his aim was merely to awaken interest in Turgenev. He freely admits that four lectures were insufficient for a satisfactory treatment, and so, implying that he does not intend to pursue the subject further, he advises his listeners and readers as to where they may find more information. Reviewing the book in *Les Nouvelles littéraires*, Edmond Jaloux praised it highly.[30] Parenthetically it is interesting to read in Maurois' journal of his return to France after World War II that during the war he lost notes for biographies of both Chekov and Tolstoy. He does not specify whether these were to have been sketches or full-length biographies, and since he did not choose to repeat his research, it is not possible to know his intentions.

It was during the same year, 1931, that Maurois published a biography of Marshal Lyautey, the French empire builder. He had known the Marshal personally for some time and greatly admired him and his achievements. In contrast with those he had already memorialized in biographies, the Marshal was not only still alive but would seem to have been a poor subject from many points of view. Maurois had reasons for thinking differently. In 1924 he had published a quasi-philosophical work called *Dialogues sur le commande-*

ment, and the questions raised in this book were to influence him heavily in his decision to write a biography of Marshal Lyautey. As the title suggests, *Dialogues* was written to provide an occasion to discuss the pros and cons of the function of command. The interlocutors are a young lieutenant in the army and his former teacher. The latter is a believer in democracy with a touch of the radical socialist in him; the former student is a believer in the command function with a touch of absolutism about his ideas. As the two men exchange opinions, the gulf between the commanding and the commanded is brought out. The lieutenant sees the need for order and control as a means to progress; the teacher is thinking mainly about the value of freedom in the absolute sense and is impatient of any and all restraints upon his liberty. The question is asked, for instance: How much credit should go to a field commander for a battle won? Do not luck, adequate support, including an able sergeant, and the particular moment in history determine the outcome of battles, rather than the skill of the general? asks the teacher. But, argues the lieutenant, persons do affect history for good and bad, as, for instance, the case of Napoleon. In more recent times the world has had Mussolini, a shrewd villain, and Hitler, a stupid one. Throughout the dialogue the teacher continues to show his fear of power. He would risk anarchy if necessary rather than yield to it.

As we now know, because Maurois has told us, the attitudes here expressed correspond in a general way to his own attitudes and to those of his teacher, Alain, but it is not necessary to assume that for this reason the dialogues are a mere reworked version of remembered conversations with his master. In fact, the suggestion by reviewers that such was the case irritated Maurois. He was also annoyed to find friends and opponents trying, on the basis of the dialogues, to identify him as a fascist or as a champion of democracy. Such attempts he repudiated:

The dialogue was between me and myself. Naturally this manoeuver was not understood. In order to blame me . . . some persons attributed to me the ideas of my philosopher, others identified me with the lieutenant and covered me with reproach along with him.[31]

Still he did remark, or permit the remark to be made in one of the dialogues, that democracy is unworkable in a backward country, and this added fuel to the flames, especially since Marshal Lyautey represented for many persons an undemocratic if not an anti-democratic force in the French army.

In turning, therefore, to the life of Lyautey for the subject of a biography, Maurois knew that he was flying in the face of many prejudices. But he admired the Marshal and regarded him as a force for progress and an agent of civilization in North Africa. The Marshal's enemies thought him an autocrat and an old-fashioned empire builder which the twentieth century must hasten to repudiate. His biographer disagreed. He had not forgotten his reception by the Marshal when he visited North Africa and the accomplishments that he had seen there. On his return home he had pictured Lyautey and his work as an example of enlightened administration. He had called this little account *Arabesques* (1925), and it was written about the same time as the *Dialogues sur le commandement*. When he began his biography of Lyautey, he incorporated into it most of this earlier study.

Marshal Lyautey's military career was fairly uneventful in its early phase like that of most peacetime colonial soldiers. As the representative of a European power, his job was to keep the peace, to "civilize the natives," and otherwise carry what was then referred to as "the white man's burden." For the soldier or officer in question this implied a series of humdrum assignments in Asia and Africa, a slow progress up the peacetime promotional ladder, and the frustration of being half way around the world from those who made the decisions. Since Lyautey was not one to let matters run their course, especially if he thought, as he usually did, that he was capable of controlling them, this meant the added frustration of having to explain frequently and humiliatingly to Paris why he had disobeyed orders. In this tug-of-war Maurois leaves no doubt as to where his sympathies lie. He supports the field commander. He prefers a benevolent dictatorship, especially when dealing with primitive peoples, to the struggle with the time-consuming and cumbersome processes of democracy. And his biography is about a man who seems to prove the validity of this political principle. Certainly throughout his career Lyautey could seldom be bothered with anyone else's point of view. He thought he was right always and, ironically, he usually was, at least from the standpoint of getting things done. Even more unpalatable to the public was the knowledge that, as an officer with royalist leanings, Lyautey despised the Third Republic that he served. Later during World War II he came to respect it more.

As it turned out, Lyautey was a failure during that war. His duties required him to cooperate with the personnel of the Ministry of

War. For the first time in years he found himself in a position where he could not command, and since he had never learned to persuade, he was doomed to failure. In "his" Morocco he could promote a sergeant to captain if he wished. He could demand the impossible and get it, and, if Maurois is to be believed, he succeeded in doing what he did without making the local people hate him and without really disturbing their way of life. From this biography the Marshal emerges as an admirable if archaic figure.

The critics were not kind to this book. Maurois was accused of hero worship, of condoning militarism and, worst of all, of writing a poor biography. From the vantage point of several decades later, this appears to be an unduly harsh judgment. Certainly the work is not dull which, considering the subject, it had a right to be. Toward the end Maurois uses the personal pronoun "I" to add authority to his view and to describe his place as an eyewitness to the events he describes. The decision to do so was injudicious. Eyewitnesses, as Maurois himself says elsewhere, are not the most impartial of biographers, and the effect of objectivity, hitherto rigorously maintained, is sacrificed to vividness. This was Maurois' first biography of a French subject, and the public wondered whether subsequent biographies would conform to this hero-worshipping pattern.

With *Edouard VII et son temps* (1933) Maurois returned to an English theme and, one suspects, to notes that he had accumulated during the writing of *Disraeli*. From the book's title arises the question as to whether he intends to write history or biography. The answer, of course, is both, but it illustrates Maurois' tendency to view history as the product of the travails and talents of men, with individuals exercising pressure on events. It is more suitable, therefore, to consider the work under the rubric of history (q.v.).

Chateaubriand (1938) was Maurois' first full-scale biography of a French literary figure. He began the work, as he had an earlier brief work on Dickens (1935), as the subject of four lectures given at the request of the Société des Conférences. Under such circumstances the treatment could not be complete, but following the advice of René Doumic, Maurois later turned his sketch into a full-length biography. There could be little doubt that the job would be well done or that it would win success with the public. Competence had already become one of his characteristics, and the great egotist was a splendid subject. When Maurois began to study Shelley, he was warned that no one in France was interested in the English poet, and so he decided to create his own public. The situation was different with Chateaubriand who is a living legend in France, even in the twentieth century.

François-René de Chateaubriand, like Byron, was profligate, even though he was less outwardly cynical. Like Byron, he was bored with life and discontented with his rather fortunate existence. He was equally fatuous and self-satisfied also, though too hypocritical to wish to appear demonic. As usual, even though his subject is less than lovable, Maurois has little difficulty in working himself up to a pitch of admiration for the man whose life he is chronicling. But the honesty that is also one of his characteristics compels him to reflect sadly from time to time on Chateaubriand's insufferable conceit and downright pomposity.

Parallel with the life of Chateaubriand, Maurois provides much insight into his literary career. We are shown among other things a man who became expert in literary craftsmanship by writing. Though he preferred grandiose ideas grandiloquently expressed to mere details, he learned even to correct proof, to substitute one word for another in his text, and to write and rewrite along with the other essential but tiresome details of the art of writing. The Chateaubriand style, we learn, did not spring full-blown from the great mind. It was cultivated and learned by long apprenticeship as was that of Balzac.

Where Chateaubriand was concerned, his tendency to see himself as the great idealist and man of principle was almost a vice. As a matter of plain fact, he was forever posing as if for a hidden camera. Silent when he should have spoken, he often rendered inaccessible thereby the glory that he wooed. The rest of the time he was scarcely at a loss for ten thousand words. By sheer tactlessness and fatuity he made a shambles of his political opportunities under Napoleon, Louis XVIII, Charles X, and Louis Philippe, yet, absurdly, he always saw his failures as the result of standing fast for principle and an unwillingness to compromise. In point of fact, he never failed to trim his sails to the least perceptible breeze if by the trimming he could make his public image more imposing.

Chateaubriand's love life, as pictured in this biography, must have been a revelation to many readers. He did not especially cultivate a reputation for chastity, and the epic of his long love for Madame Récamier is well known, but to learn that, like Hugo, he was an insatiable and even ridiculous sensualist must come as something of a surprise. The sum total is a fascinating little man with a gigantic ego, a genius whose greatest work was a lengthy autobiography—

an autobiography in which, even as his admirers know, the pictures are posed, the truths manipulated, and the emotions calculated. Posterity is hard on Chateaubriand and may continue to be so, but this is not Maurois' doing. His biography is a straightforward record concerning this least straightforward of records.

IV   *Biographies of the Post-War Period*

His study of Chateaubriand later led Maurois quite naturally into the study of his equally fascinating female contemporary, Aurore Dupin, whose masculine pseudonym, George Sand, tells posterity more about her than she intended. The work, entitled *Lélia* (1952), appeared after a lapse of more than fourteen years during which time no major biography had come from Maurois' pen. The task that he undertook, in resuming his biographical researches, was as difficult from most points of view as his work on Chateaubriand. The vastness of George Sand's correspondence equals if it does not exceed Chateaubriand's, and the number, variety, and eminence of her acquaintances reveal an existence that touched most of the great men of her day. Even a partial roster of her friends is startling to say the least. Among them were Chopin, Liszt, Musset, Vigny, Hugo, Sainte-Beuve, Dumas, Flaubert, the Goncourt brothers, Turgenev, and Lamartine. In addition to these men, whom she knew intimately, there was a secondary group, few of them well known today, but all of them picturesque and interesting as human beings. She was also well acquainted with all the rulers of France during her lifetime, including the two Napoleons.

Central to any account of George Sand's life is the question of her immorality or amorality. Her lovers were many, and Maurois, in the fulfilment of his duty as a biographer, chronicles the love affairs which followed each other with almost monotonous regularity. Yet he is able to make out a fair case for thinking Madame Sand a chaste woman at heart, or at least chaste in her attitude toward love. In each successive love affair she hoped to find the great, sincere passion of her life, and though she never succeeded, she never lost faith in love.

No less complex was the task of evaluating Madame Sand's more than sixty novels, the good ones and the bad ones that flowed from her pen at the unvarying rate of twenty pages a day despite amours, travels, or revolution. As in Chateaubriand's case, not the least of her literary endeavors was her unending attempt to shape her autobiography to her satisfaction. In this she succeeded as little as did

Chateaubriand in telling a story that remotely resembles the truth, but at least her intentions were more honest than his. She did not consciously lie, but she continued to revise and rework the "truth" in order to make it reflect as accurately as possible her changing views and her increasing sagacity about persons and ideas. The task of the biographer is thereby rendered Herculean, but Maurois has managed quite successfully to untangle the skein of George Sand's existence. He depicts also those whose lives were intermingled with hers, while keeping his heroine to the fore. At the same time the pageant of the times is constantly in view.

What Maurois' biography has succeeded in accomplishing is nothing less than a rehabilitation of Madame Sand's character. He says in his introduction that unlike most previous biographers, who found it amusing to treat her with cruelty and irony, he has the peculiarity of liking her, and that his book is written out of sympathy and affection as well as from the point of view of historical interest. For years tender-minded readers and critics were more repelled by George Sand's hypocrisy, as they called it, than by the frank de-monism of Byron or the carefully posed piety of Chateaubriand. This is not to imply that Maurois would have us condone her obvious breaches of morality and good taste. He criticizes her, for instance, for letting her children travel about with her as she pursued her amorous adventures, only to be chagrined when her daughter, admiring her mother's conduct, began to emulate it.

Some special pleading is found in this biography, but by frequent interruption of the narrative with passages from Madame Sand's letters the reader is enabled to contrast Maurois' interpretation with the facts as his subject saw them. After we have read her own words, her hatreds may still seem detestable, her violence repugnant, and her quarrels banal, but we are bound to acquire some insight into her mind. And all that we find there is not unworthy of respect. We may dismiss most of Sand's novels as the product of a prolific but not brilliant talent, as it is currently the fashion to do, but we should at least heed Maurois when he says that at her best she is very good indeed.

As might be expected, George Sand was far from orthodox in religion. In her latter years she was easy prey to a quack named Leroux who preached a kind of faith healing. Her misplaced con-fidence in him led her to refuse an operation that might have saved her life. Because conscience was a strong element in her ethics, she displayed courage in admitting mistakes. In fact, so tortured was

Madame Sand's exaggerated sincerity that she was unable to bear for an instant the thought that she had wronged anyone, intentionally or otherwise. Her friends knew this and esteemed her accordingly. From the names of her friends and enemies one can compile a useful index to her character. To have been the friend of Flaubert, to have been disliked by Baudelaire and admired by Anatole France is no mean distinction. And if, as alleged, Sainte-Beuve never dared to print what he actually thought of her, this is for George Sand an added kudo and but another proof of the critic's occasional discretion.

Maurois has deftly handled the thousands of documents that include the misleading and fiendishly long autobiography. From his account we glimpse a real person, one who, if not capable of arousing all our respect, is at least entitled to a measure of our sympathy. But in this Maurois has the defects of his qualities, and his penchant for interrupting his narrative to include scores of letters, many of them useful, but many of them trivial and wordy, is occasionally overindulged. The letters sometimes tell the story far less well than the biographer is capable of doing. In some chapters quotation reaches the point where the text consists mainly of citations loosely held together by a few sentences of explanation. Yet Maurois regarded this as essential. He felt it his duty to make the fullest possible use of the documents that came his way, and, as he explains in his introduction, he was fortunate enough to have access to documents never before used in writing Madame Sand's life. These he felt he must use, and if the result is a narrative that suffers from interruptions more than his other biographies, it must also be added that this biography is, to a greater extent than the others, an original contribution to our knowledge of its subject.

The publication of *Olympio, ou la vie de Victor Hugo* in 1954 might have been expected to add nothing new to Maurois' reputation as a biographer. Once again, however, he applied the techniques of careful research and attention to detail, and the resulting biography is excellent. Here, as elsewhere, he frequently relies on the anecdote or spicy incident for his effects. The result is splendid from the point of view of the reader's enjoyment, but it must be mentioned that Maurois has sometimes been accused of preferring such tales to less striking but more characteristic events. In other words, he is said to enjoy telling the kind of charming and possibly apocryphal stories about his heroes that have long plagued the biographers of George Washington. Yet every hero has his cherry tree, and such tales have an irresistible appeal for the reader. If judiciously used, they contribute enormously to our pleasure. *Ariel*, of course, is what it is precisely because of such tales. Later on, the caution of middle years caused Maurois to warn his readers to take such stories with a grain of salt, but to the historian's dismay and the reader's delight he continues to use them. *Olympio* is no exception.

As usual, the biographer spares the reader none of the details of his subject's love life. When, as is the case with Hugo, the subject was one of the great sensualists of all time, the result is an intimate and detailed portrait that is likely to repel prudish readers. The sight, for instance, of Hugo setting out to debauch a young girl when he was well past his eightieth birthday is a trifle unappetizing, and when we add the fact that Hugo, with his insufferable egotism, thought he was conferring a favor on the object of his attentions, the scene is decidedly unpleasant.

But to speak of this is to anticipate a little. Hugo was before all else, even before sensuality, a poet, and there are Frenchmen who can wax lyric in admiration of nearly every line of the hundreds of thousands he wrote. To admire him is as truly French as to admire Racine, for the French can bear the egomania of a poet if his poetry is worth reading. Americans with their Anglo-Saxon reticence, on the other hand, are likely to find Hugo's posturings, such as are found in his famous "Tristesse d'Olympio," a little silly. For this reason the Hugo of the *cénacles*, and the Hugo of *Hernani* and *Ruy Blas* is easier for foreigners to understand and admire than the egotist of *La Légende des siècles* or even the *Art d'être un grandpère*. This does not imply, I think, that we are not epic-minded or that we do not idolize our children. But there is something faintly odious to Anglo-Saxons in the pose of the one collection and the sentimentality of the other. We greatly prefer the vituperation of *Les Châtiments*. Hugo's enemy Sainte-Beuve, the suborner of his wife's affections, was, for all his mealy-mouthed hypocrisy, preferable in some ways to the self-righteous Hugo. The latter was too conceited even to realize that he was a hypocrite. Maurois knows all these things, but he also knows that he is writing a biography primarily for a nation that adores Hugo.

The domestic scenes of Hugo's life are well done as are those of his public life. The poetry is dealt with satisfactorily as are the prose works and the plays, and such is the power of biography with its sympathetic treatment of a life that all readers are able to rejoice in the genius of Hugo. There were few dissenting voices among the enthusiastic readers of *Olympio* either in France or abroad. With one accord it was praised as a great biography.

In 1966 Maurois published in France, and in English translation, some carefully chosen excerpts from *Olympio* with copious illustrations, thereby providing admirers of Hugo and students of French literature with an unusual picture book for the study of the poet's life and times. The shorter work, entitled *Victor Hugo*, condenses the biography from more than four hundred pages to something over one hundred forty, of which more than half are illustrations.

Les Trois Dumas (1957) is a welcome relief from the sober atmosphere of the *Hugo*. Our biographer writes of the same period and deals with some of the same people, but little else is the same. The Dumas family had an energy and vigor in their character that make even the lusty Hugo pale by comparison. All three of the Dumas are prime biographic material. From the gigantic general, a muscular colossus who was an unsuccessful politician, to the equally robust immoralist known as Alexandre Dumas père, and the more esthetic grandson who was a dramatist, a progression appears which is in its every aspect a fascinating story. Least well told is the story of Alexander the first. The account of his life opens the volume, but though our imagination is at once aroused by his personality and his deeds, our biographer drops him too quickly to satisfy his readers. As one finishes this portion of the book, he feels that the career of this first Dumas during the Revolution and Empire is still to be told. He appears at the beginning as an ancestor often does in order to throw light upon the birth, the surroundings, and character of the real subject of the biography; then, after we have been given but slightly more information than would be necessary if the title were *Les Deux Dumas*, he is allowed to disappear, and we begin the biography proper, which is that of the novelist.

Alexandre Dumas père is a biographer's dream, for his qualities were as varied as his adventures. There are hardly enough adjectives in the rich French language to describe him: prodigal, sensual, creative, generous, humorous, impractical, only begin a list of descriptive words which could and does go on and on as Maurois tells his life story. And as the mind occasionally recoils in distaste from the megalomania of a Hugo, a Chateaubriand, a Byron, or a George Sand, it accepts and even revels in the incredible exploits of Alexandre Dumas. He is successively Gargantua, Tom Jones, and Sancho Panza. The extent of his genius and his ability to write not dozens but hundreds of pages in a brief space of time are little short of unbelievable. The same may be said for his inability to hold on to the vast sums of money that came to him. But his loves and his laughter are memorable, and Maurois makes his reader like the hulking immoralist and even admire him.

Maurois had a more difficult time of it with the third Dumas. Alexandre Dumas fils was a brave, talented and self-contained man. He was also a bitter one. He was bitter, first of all, toward his father for raising him in the midst of a flagrant and unashamed immorality. He was bitter toward the world for having tolerated that immorality, and he was even more bitter toward women for allowing men, like himself, to behave in an immoral way. For the younger Dumas, though not a chaste man, thoroughly disapproved of his own conduct. The problem of conscience versus conduct is a complex one, and our biographer has disposed of it rather too summarily. As a result, the younger Dumas as presented is fairly unpalatable. A longer treatment might have explained more, and, with more explanation, the reader might have acquired more sympathy for him.

Taken altogether, this biographical trilogy must be regarded as a one-third success. As originally published, as the life of the novelist alone, the book had a tremendous and well deserved popularity and received broadly based critical acclaim. The critic of the *Atlantic Monthly*, for instance, had this to say about it:

> [It is] a work as solid and distinguished as its predecessors, *Lélia* and *Olympio*, and enthrallingly readable. To those who especially relish the flamboyant, it should prove the most attractive of M. Maurois' books, for flamboyant is certainly the operative word for the Dumas.[32]

Henri Peyre of Yale, by no means consistently kind to Maurois in his reviews, also liked the book immensely.[33] Unfortunately it was only as a kind of afterthought or sequel that Maurois decided to add a generation at each end. The result is an uneven work, for while Dumas the novelist properly takes the center of the stage, the briefer treatment of his father and of his son give an impression of haste and skimpiness. For best reading, therefore, the one-volume life of Dumas père is to be preferred. Its pages sparkle with life and wit, and within its covers move the host of great and little men of those stirring times. It is difficult to realize that these are also the days of the pompous Hugo and the troubled George Sand. How dull are her adulteries in contrast with infidelities of Dumas! Nor does Maurois alone make the difference. The difference lies in Dumas himself.

He lived such a life that those who came after him can hardly make the telling of it dull even if they try, which assuredly Maurois does not do. It was, of course, no accident that Maurois was well informed about the period. By choosing to write successively about persons living in the same era, the information gleaned in writing about each one was useful in writing about the rest. Thus, as Maurois proceeds, he is ever better informed about the first decades of the nineteenth century.

V   *The Last Biographies*

If a biography of Dumas was easy to write, Maurois' next biography, *La Vie de Sir Alexander Fleming* (1959) was not. To write it at all was a *tour de force,* or so it seemed to Maurois, though he has never used that exact expression about it. When asked by Lady Fleming to write a biography of her husband, he was somewhat taken aback. He had never before attempted to chronicle the life of a scientist. Still he saw a certain poetic justice in being asked to write a biography of a real-life Scot, for he had begun his writing career by telling the story of an imaginary one in *Les Silences du Colonel Bramble.* When he finally agreed to write about Fleming, Maurois turned for a while away from the Romantic period with its adulterers and egotistical geniuses to deal with a chaste and genuinely modest man of science. In so doing, he produced one of his most human biographies. The achievement is all the more remarkable when one realizes that a case can be made for the essential dullness of Dr. Fleming and the pedestrian nature of the day-to-day laboratory work which, after years of plodding, led to one of the great discoveries of science.

One of the first facts that we learn about Dr. Fleming from Maurois' account is that he was a taciturn man, so taciturn that to many of his associates he seemed dour, a quality often attributed, rightly or wrongly, to the Scottish nation. Maurois is so aware of his subject's wordlessness that he feels it necessary to reassure the reader time and again that his hero is not the gloomy Scot that he appears on the surface but a sensitive, likeable, sportsloving, and funloving man who was simply not articulate about his feelings. The reader is finally convinced that such was the case, but it requires all Maurois' skill to make the point.

It was Fleming's taciturnity, or a form of it, which almost prevented him from becoming well known. We are astonished to learn that after his discovery of penicillin he allowed ten years to elapse before taking effective steps to assure its production. One cannot help but reflect upon what another Alexander, the Frenchman Dumas, would have done under similar circumstances. Would he not have turned out reams of copy? But Fleming contented himself with quietly calling attention to his discovery from time to time, always with a modest reminder that it might some day be found useful. His failure to act was caused, at least in part, by his fanatical devotion to the director of his laboratory, Almroth Wright, a bitter, sarcastic Irishman who urged caution upon him and kept the discovery bottled up. Wright's influence was destructive, and all Fleming's devotion to him and all Maurois' skill in explaining him cannot make him likeable or even bearable.

Fleming, as we come to know him, is what foreigners like to think of as the typical Britisher, a man who works hard all day, plays some game or other at his club over a pint of ale when the day is over, and then, after hours, relaxes with his family during the long British weekends. Fleming fitted all these stereotypes. He also smoked incessantly, but he had few other conspicuous habits. He is strange stuff for a hero, but he is far more akin to the men of this century than the undisciplined and exuberant intellectuals of the Romantic period. His was an almost monastic life. It was all the more remarkable, therefore, that when honors finally came to him, he transformed himself into a traveling ambassador for British science, blossoming forth to everyone's delight and surprise as an articulate and witty speaker on all kinds of subjects. All this in a biography makes good reading, and Maurois need not have feared this trial of his powers. He was more than equal to the task. Science and Fleming live in these pages.

In 1961 appeared *Adrienne,* a life of the Marquise de Lafayette. Maurois felt strongly that the famous Marquis, a hero in the American Revolution, had already had more than his legitimate share of fame, and so he set out to chronicle the life story of his long-suffering and distinguished wife who is virtually unknown to the public. The biography that resulted is excellent, though for the first hundred pages the more famous husband manages to steal the limelight, a feat that he seems as capable of repeating in his wife's biography as in real life. It is only after the Marquis has been placed in an Austrian prison that our biographer manages to keep our attention focused upon Adrienne and to enable us to find her admirable. It was she who undertook to free her husband, and she who rebuilt the family fortune after Lafayette got out of prison. It was she who

hobbled about on an infected leg doing the errands required to re-
cover the family social and financial position. But she was less
pathetic in her suffering than the husband who was so fatuously and
callously unaware of the extent of his wife's pain and sacrifice. His
selfish willingness to let her destroy the last remnants of her health
in his service while by letters and memoranda he nagged her for her
failures and withheld praise for her partial successes is hard to forgive. This was the Marquis' least attractive side.

The qualities that make Adrienne a great woman are less flashy
and, therefore, less commonly noticed than the dash and the physical
courage that made the public of two continents love her husband.
Madame de Lafayette, by way of contrast, was modest, affectionate,
and charitable. Her moral courage equalled her husband's physical
courage, and by sharing his dungeon in Austria she proved that she
possessed the latter quality also. Her selflessness was constantly high-
lighted by her husband's contrasting egotism, her chastity by his
childish unfaithfulness. Through well chosen letters we are shown the
intimate details of their married life, and we conclude sadly that the
wife's is the nobler role. She, too, loved decency and liberty, but she
sought to influence her times by actions rather than words. In contrast, Lafayette's posturing on the subject of liberty—sincere though
his basic commitment was, his eternal willingness to involve himself
in controversy when to do so was not only reckless but useless—
makes him an attractive but impractical hero. Madame de Lafayette
was a heroine without the necessity of qualification. Yet Maurois is
no one-sided biographer. He knows his craft too well for that. He
knows also that whatever his faults, and they were many, Lafayette
was an authentic hero in his own right. Still, to gloss over as somehow
pardonable the Marquis' calm resumption of his relationship with
his mistress after his wife had spent four years in prison with him
seems somehow a bit too charitable.

The end of the story, with its poignant account of Adrienne's death
as told by her husband, is a remarkable document. If it does not
excuse, it extenuates to a degree the general's conduct. Adrienne is a
true heroine as well as wife and mother. She deserved this biography.

Maurois' most recent biography is that of Balzac, which he entitled, not inappropriately, *Prométhée* (1965). He said that it would
be his last. French critical comment has been both favorable and
unfavorable. Nor is there unanimity in the American and British
reviews. Francis Steegmuller in the *New York Times* had high praise
for the book, saying that it proved once again that Maurois was the

greatest living French literary biographer.[34] Writing in "Book Week" in the *Washington Post* Leo Bersani is less sure. After declaring the biography a "fitting finale to a distinguished career," he goes on to find it lacking in certain elements. He thinks that Maurois should have interpreted Balzac's life differently, for he sees Balzac's conservative ideology as a "protection against a fantastic imagination for chaos . . ."[35] (whatever that means).

As usual, Maurois tells a good story. The readers of the biography are made to see all of Balzac. In his life story he appears, as he does in all workmanlike accounts of his life, as that *enfant terrible* of the real world who in his fiction was the unaccountably sensible and shrewd creator of shrewd and sensible characters. He who made fun in his novels of dupes who bought junk under the delusion that they were buying art treasures was himself a collector of junk. He who knew how to make the fortunes of his characters with well placed investments was incredibly naïve about his own investments. He who understood human nature well enough to create and to motivate a dazzling variety of human types was in real life unable to get along with his own mother and sister. In real life Balzac was a *petit bourgeois* with a touch of vulgarity about him. As a novelist, he surmounted class distinctions. The copy that he turned out, working at night, was always written under forced draft because of his habit of demanding payment for unwritten novels and spending the money as soon as he got it. And so, because of his prodigal ways, he had to work without respite, ruining his eyes and his health in the process.

In one field only do we find the Balzac who wrote the novels not inferior to the characters that he created, and that is in the domain of amours. Ugly though Balzac was, frequently unkempt, and even actually dirty about his person, he could attract and hold the affection of women, and the love life of this man who never permitted personal relations to interfere with his daily stint of writing is a fascinating tale. There is also something touching and childlike about Balzac's way of mistaking imagination for reality, for without this trait he could not have written the *Comédie humaine*. At the same time it was this trait which was to make his life frequently unhappy. Yet he was ever the incurable optimist who thought that his next speculation was going to make him rich. And, *mirabile dictu*, some of those who tried out the schemes which he simply dreamed of succeeded beyond his wildest hopes.

One sees little or no diminution in Maurois' powers in this last of his biographies. Balzac has been written about before and will surely by written about again, but Maurois' book will be one to reckon with. Its chief flaw is that habit of excessive documentation which has been with him since he wrote *Lélia*. This detracts at times from the story he is telling and telling well. Much of the material is presented in the form of citations from the subject's correspondence, a procedure which insures a rigid adherence to the facts. Balzac is made thereby to draw his own portrait. But, as was the case in the biography of George Sand, the many quotations in certain chapters resemble mere scholarly impedimenta which come between the biographer and his subject. At times even the thread of the narrative is obscured by these interruptions, until the reader is tempted to skip the citations and to confine his attention to Maurois' text. Still, everything considered, the story is well told. With half the quotations it would be told better. But as Maurois says, after his Shelley was attacked by "fools," he determined if necessary to overdo the scholarly apparatus.

VI *Short Biographies*

Little known and deserving of a better fate are three short biographies: that of Voltaire, that of Joseph Smith, and that of Harry Truman. Jean Prévost thought the first of these well written, the "best thing that he has done," and he wonders at Maurois' own timidity in referring to it.[36] The second, concerning Joseph Smith, is little more than a preliminary sketch, for Maurois, at the request of the Church of Latter-Day Saints (Mormon), gave up his plans for a full-scale, scholarly biography of the founder of Mormonism. The Truman biography, a brief (57 quarto pages), business-like account of the former American president's life, has never appeared in book form.

Short biographical vignettes have also attracted Maurois' attention and have claimed a good share of his time. In some cases he may have been simply making an exploratory study with a view to undertaking a full-length biography later on. But in many cases it is plain that he had neither the wish nor the intent to go any further than the sketch itself. Most of these he gathered together in two collections, *Magiciens et logiciens* (1935) and *Destins exemplaires* (1952). Both collections partake of literary criticism as well as biography and must therefore be considered from both points of view. He has published many other sketches separately or in collections whose contents have been shuffled and reshuffled in successive editions.

Among the Frenchmen he has treated are distinguished contemporaries, others are close personal friends. Some answer to both descriptions. They include his old teacher Alain, the subject of two essays, Balzac, Barrès, Charles Du Bos, Simone de Beauvoir, Jean-Paul Sartre, Thierry de Martel, Jean Prévost, Napoleon, Adelbert Quesnay, Sainte-Beuve, Saint-Exupéry, Vauvenargues, and Vigny. In all these sketches, whether he is writing of someone well known to history, like Napoleon, or of a personal friend, like Charles Du Bos, he strives, generally with success, to tell a good story, enlivened with anecdotes and free of the baggage of scholarship. Just as in short story writing there is no room for the leisurely descriptions and lengthy character developments of the novel, so in the biographical vignette the technique of the long biography must change. Unnecessary sentences and the luxury of proceeding slowly to a climax have to be avoided. And it must be said that Maurois excels in the art of the short biography no less than in the writing of the long one. In each case the reader is led to believe that he knows the subject of the sketch intimately even though in point of fact he has barely met him.

If we sort out the non-French subjects by nationality, we see that Maurois has sketched the lives of four Russians, three Germans, thirteen Englishmen, and two Americans. There is also one Italian and one Spaniard.

The Russians whom he chose to delineate, in addition to Turgenev, are Gogol, Chekov, and Tolstoy. It was in part the preparation for the Turgenev lectures that turned Maurois' attention to Russia, but he tells us that he turned to the reading of Chekov at the suggestion of his friend Maurice Baring. The Chekov portrait is a memorable one. In a few pages we see the tubercular but always cheerful Russian pursuing his two careers, medicine and writing. In Gogol we see the self-tortured and unhappy writer, turning away from the work that is his salvation to seek satisfaction in a self-induced and almost hallucinatory mysticism. The Tolstoy sketch describes the Russian's rejection of his wife in favor of an unrealizable spirituality. This sketch was aptly entitled *Léon Tolstoy et le bonheur conjugal.*

Among the great Germans he chose three: Goethe, Kleist, and Beethoven, each one in marked contrast to the other two. Goethe, the Olympian, with his talent, his success, and his self-confidence is at opposite poles from Kleist, the half-mad, unhappy poet, yet each subject is portrayed with equal skill and with equal sympathy. The sketch of Beethoven was contributed to a collective work about the musician in which musicologists as well as literary men are represented. The book was intended as a contribution to knowledge, and not merely as another beautiful volume for display on the library table, although certainly it is that also. Maurois was asked to address himself to the seemingly frivolous task of telling the story of Beethoven's love life, but in his hands the love stories are worth the telling. Rejecting from the outset any trivial or facetious approach, Maurois documents in a scholarly but by no means boring way Beethoven's experiences with women. He tells what they meant to him in the way of happiness and, above all, what they contributed to his music.

Like the French sketches, Maurois' English ones are divided among great writers of the past and distinguished contemporaries. In alphabetical order the writers memorialized are: Maurice Baring, James Boswell, Elizabeth and Robert Browning, G. K. Chesterton, Joseph Conrad, Aldous Huxley, Rudyard Kipling, D. H. Lawrence, Katherine Mansfield, William Shakespeare, G. B. Shaw, Lytton Strachey, and H. G. Wells. Whenever possible, as in the case of Kipling and in that of Maurice Baring, both of whom he knew intimately, he stands quite ready to show the extent of his affection and respect for his subject as he pens a portrait for posterity. In such cases, although he remains an analyst of character, Maurois is as interested in creating a favorable impression as in presenting an objective picture.

If Maurois had searched long and hard for two more contrasting American figures, he could not have found them. Ernest Hemingway and Emily Dickinson were about as far apart as two human beings can be, but each of them becomes a knowable person for the French reader in his sketches. Emily the recluse, with her quiet, feminine ways and her preoccupation with death, is sympathetically and lovingly described, while Papa Hemingway, with his *bonhomie* and brutality, is no less well presented. It is as if Maurois asked himself whether, like Milton, he could be equally successful with *L'Allegro* and *Il Penseroso*, and to everyone's satisfaction he was.

In each of these biographical vignettes, whatever the time, place, or the nationality of the subject, each one is deftly placed in his own milieu, and one feels neither estrangement nor strangeness in moving from Wimpole Street, London, to Amherst, Massachusetts, or from Frankfurt, Germany, to old Saint Petersburg, Russia. No one manages the rapid creation of milieux and atmosphere so well as Maurois. He is particularly interested as few adults are in the rebellion of young people against their environment. He tries to understand those who feel themselves misunderstood, and to make their problems comprehensible. He never permits himself or his readers a smirk of self-righteousness as he observes the trials and tribulations of young genius. There but for the grace of God, he seems to say, go you and I.

The treatment of such historical figures as Shakespeare, Voltaire, and Napoleon is inevitably more philosophical. The sketch of Shakespeare tries to show, not too successfully, that the tragedies, like most great art, were a product of personal griefs and sorrows. The brief Balzac, surprisingly enough, ends with the opinion that the novelist is greater than Shakespeare.

During the course of his career Maurois has frequently written biographies for children. The first of these was a brief account of the life of Chopin (1942). During the war years, when he was domiciled in the United States, he wrote a book on the sculptor J. L. David, which was followed by illustrated lives of Washington, Franklin, and Eisenhower. Sometime after his return to France he wrote *Lafayette in America* (1952), and a year later he wrote *Cecil Rhodes*, the story of the South African empire builder. In all these books Maurois succeeds rather well in capturing the flavor of the times, just as he does in his adult biographies. He also presents authentic heroes of the sort children like, but his simplifications are never puerile. And though his children's biographies are intended to edify as well as to inform and amuse, they are not overly sententious. It must be admitted, however, that Maurois is an indefatigable moralist. In his memoirs he confesses that when his children were young, he exercised a rather strict control over them, and so his biographies, like his rearing of his children, are in the French tradition.

It may also be surmised without invidiousness that the *Lafayette* and the *Chopin* were by-products of spade work that he had been doing on his biography of Madame de Lafayette and George Sand respectively.

VII *The Biographer Looks at His Role*

Maurois' work as a biographer is vast in bulk. It represents an enormous amount of study and reflection. It is also obvious that he enjoyed the work quite aside from its part in creating for him an international reputation. This reputation is undoubtedly durable, requiring no bolstering, explanations or self-analysis from the biographer. But obviously, too, Maurois enjoys the role of explicator of his own aims and methods. He was pleased, therefore, when an opportunity for public self-evaluation of his biographical method was afforded him in 1928 by an invitation from Trinity College, Cambridge, to give the Clark Lectures. As a topic he chose "Aspects of Biography," and the essay produced from his lectures was an altogether solid and substantial discussion of an important phase of his career.

For his audience Maurois explored most phases of biographical writing. He asks, among other things, whether an autobiography is actually "truer" than a biography, and concludes that it is not necessarily so. It is possible for a man who tells his own story to misunderstand, misrepresent, or forget important aspects of his life. This is why the objective biographer may sometimes describe a subject far better than he can possibly describe himself. Maurois tries to demonstrate that, contrary to popular opinion, the so-called romanced biography, in which the writer puts words into the mouth of his hero, may not distort reality. The words ascribed to the subject may, in fact, represent him, for they can be taken from letters and other documents which show plainly that he held the views attributed to him. It is sometimes permissible, therefore, to attribute conversations to a subject when we know that he has expressed the same ideas in essentially the same way at the same period of his life. Maurois asked his audience the perennial question: "What is truth?" and then wondered aloud, as it were, whether a biographer ever had the right to suppress the truth. He shows conclusively that the writing of a biography is not very far from the process of writing a novel, since both require the exercise of judgment as to what is to go into the final version. Obviously, one cannot put in all that is known. The biographer or novelist must choose among the available anecdotes, documents, and letters, and in choosing he inevitably creates a certain image of the subject, an image which may not in the least resemble that which would have been created if other equally valid anecdotes, documents, and letters had been presented instead of those actually chosen.

While pretending that he had no intention of taking time for a résumé of the art of biography in Britain, Maurois did, in effect, provide such a résumé. He praises Lytton Strachey, whom he credits with having made an art out of the biographical *genre*. He turns next to the importance of the choice of subject. Biography, he thinks, must not become a disguised form of hero-worship. The biographer must remain impartial. Yet if he is to do a competent piece of work, it is inadvisable to attempt the biography of someone he actively dislikes. He must also face the fact that his attitude toward his subject is likely to change several times in the course of his research and writing. He also made it plain that he takes the task of biographer seriously and that he regards it as a legitimate form of literary endeavor. Scholarship is a part of it, and he says that when he began his work on Shelley, he neither knew nor appreciated either its importance or its methods. In the preparation for his second book he was initiated into its mysteries, and since then he has tried to practice its rites. In short, there were few aspects of the art of biography that Maurois did not cover in these lectures, and the glimpse into his working habits it most enlightening.

Evidently Maurois was not altogether satisfied that he had said all that he meant to say in the Clark Lectures. Accordingly he prefaced his study of Marcel Proust in the *Oeuvres complètes* with some additional remarks on the value and method of autobiography. He repeats his conviction that an entirely "sincere" autobiography is impossible. Not only does the self that one sets out to describe change from year to year and even from hour to hour, but there is always the danger that once a person has crystallized himself in an autobiography, he will unconsciously strive thereafter to imitate the stereotype that he has created. He will never be quite himself again. Life in such a situation may imitate art. For this reason he feels that an autobiography that comments profusely on other persons, persons whom the author has met and admired, or known and hated, is more likely to be true to some essential aspect of the writer's life than one that deals almost exclusively with himself. He feels for this same reason that a novel into which the writer puts a great deal of himself, although unconsciously, may reveal him more accurately and completely than his autobiography. Despite these reservations, he wrote the story of his life.

CHAPTER 4

Bright Pages of History

MANY assiduous readers of Maurois who are fairly well acquainted with the ensemble of his work as a novelist and
biographer are less well read in his historical studies. The writing
of history was, for Maurois, by no means an afterthought. It would
perhaps have been far more surprising if he had chosen not to write
history. It is amusing to note in retrospect that Jean Prévost, writing
in the *La Nouvelle Revue Française*, suggested in a long article on
Maurois that it was quite likely that he would one day be writing
history as a logical progression in his career. A few months later he
obliged by publishing his *Histoire d'Angleterre* (1937).

I *An Amateur Historian*

As has already been noted, Maurois appears at all times to have
been reluctant not to make full use in one way or another of all the
materials that his study and research have furnished him. It was
impossible for him to delve into the lives of literary figures of at
least three centuries without becoming intimately acquainted with
the main historical outlines of the periods in question. It was similarly
unthinkable for him, impeccable stylist that he is, to have been satisfied with history as he found it expounded in the books that he had
to study. Until recently, with the notable exceptions whose fame is
universal—Voltaire, Gibbon, and a few others—historical writing
has lagged behind other literary forms in readability and ease of
presentation. It is only in our own times that the professional historian has come to deem it his duty to write well, perhaps even enter-
tainingly. Inevitably the thought must have occurred to Maurois that
with some effort on his part he might increase the popular appeal
of historical writing and perhaps even make of it an art form.

The result of his decision to write history has been criticized from
two opposing quarters. Critics of his novels feel that he should not

have strayed from the field of fiction. Professional historians were also ready with their barbs, attacking him as a popularizer. Maurois expected this to happen. He had already experienced this kind of reproach with regard to his biographies, and for this reason he determined to make his history as accurate and as professional as possible. At the same time he was careful to avoid any claim of originality. He wrote in the preface to his *Histoire des Etats-Unis:*

America has had remarkable historians, and today she has more than ever. I have read many of them. I have tried to extract the essential from their works and to present the facts as clearly as possible.[37]

He also believed that one of the useful qualities of his books was that in them the French reader will find many important documents translated into French for the first time. These claims are modest, and from them has resulted the additional criticism that he has been too modest in his purpose: if he proposed no more than this, he need not have written history at all. Evidently there were some who were determined to find fault.

A second and important aspect of Maurois' decision to write history in a serious and professional manner was his oft expressed conviction that history is made by men. He does not believe it to be the blind result of unchanging and unchangeable forces working toward a foreordained end. He believes that individuals in strategic positions are able to influence the course of events for good or evil. The importance of biography is thereby proved, and for this reason also some of his novels are little more than disguised biographies. For Maurois the individual is crucial. He does not hold to the deterministic view that if Louis XIV, Disraeli, Churchill, or Hitler had not lived, the same inexorable processes, working through different men, would have achieved the same ends. History, for him, is what men have made it. It represents our triumphs and failures, and our progress toward a humane civilization. It reflects as well the human tendency to backslide into barbarism. Our collective salvation or destruction, therefore, will result from the actions of outstanding men. Maurois is specific about this. When he had decided to write a history of France he said that he was about to compose a continuous story with portraits. In other words, he could not conceive of history without biographical sketches. Everywhere in history he has glimpsed the presence of men, changing the course of nations and, with them, the course of destiny. Some of the men were outstanding in good, others outstanding in evil, but good or evil it is they who have created what the superstitious call "fate." As a biographer this meant for Maurois that a Byron, however moved by destructive and mutually antagonistic forces within him, could not blame his actions on God or the Devil, or blind fate. He was responsible.

Such a view of persons and their role in life is an important one for an historian, whether one agrees with it or not, since a history written by a hero-worshipper, if that is not too strong a term, will differ from that written by a determinist. One of the ramifications of this theory as to the importance of individuals is to the effect that fools and weak men, at crucial moments in history, have been no less influential than have geniuses and intellectuals. Weak men by what they fail to do affect history as decisively as do the virtuous. The oft-repeated message of Maurois as an historian is this: we who dwell upon this planet make life what it is. By the interplay of individual wills, actions, hopes, and strivings occur the sequences of events that we call "history." He notes with interest the dictum of Pascal that a change in the length of Cleopatra's nose might have changed the history of Western Europe. Yet, for Maurois, Cleopatra's nose simply was what it was. If he has sometimes amused himself with rewriting history according to Pascal's view, he has done so mainly with satiric intent.[38] His candid view is, apparently, that the chief lesson of history is that there are no lessons from history. Speaking of the two World Wars he says:

Mainly I then believed that by throwing light on past mistakes there was a possibility of turning men away from future ones. I was mistaken. One cannot wash twice in the same water. History does not permit one to foresee the future. But it teaches, as Alain says, that the most important secret of life is to expect what one has not foreseen.[39]

A possible implication of the idea that each man is responsible for himself might be to justify the castigation of those whose influence is bad, and whose actions have damaged the collective well-being. This Maurois does not do. For though a man is by no means destined to be a Puritan or a libertine, and though his individual choice is free, still he is what he is, and casting opprobrium upon him for the fact is the most futile of futile exercises. Maurois has none of the reformer's zeal to change what has been. He is never tempted to rewrite history in order to give it the complexion that he would like it to have. His disclaimer on this point is clear: "I have never allowed myself to bend the facts of history, to deform or to rearrange them in order to support my personal views. I have no thesis to defend." [40]

Most of these attitudes toward life and history Maurois has made known directly in his prefaces as well as in scattered essays. All of them are well documented by implication in his novels, biographies, and miscellaneous writings. It is no surprise, therefore, to find him displaying the same qualities as he turns to the role of historian.

There was a reason for turning first to the history of Britain. From the outset of his writing career, after spending the war years as a liaison officer with a British unit, Maurois decided to continue in a civilian capacity the task to which he was assigned in the army, that is, to interpret the French to the British, and *vice versa*. He realized at the time of his first exposure to Anglo-Saxon ways just how little one who lived less than one hundred miles from England knew of her culture, her mores, and her history. His personal discovery was to the effect that a great reservoir of good will lay in Britain, and a cultural tradition worth knowing. Above all there were in Britain human beings of an infinite and delightful variety, and he determined to make it his business for the rest of his life to combat French ignorance on this score. To this end the writing of history was a useful weapon in his arsenal. He had come to see for himself the value of a broad outlook, and he wished in the best interest of his compatriots to combat French ignorance and provincialism.

The *Histoire d'Angleterre* first appeared in 1937, since which time it has been reissued at various times, culminating in a definitive edition brought up to date as of 1963. For the task which he set himself, Maurois expected to use all available authorities, and one senses from the tone and style of his historical writing that he is seldom far removed from his card file or more than an hour away from a library. All the usual scholarly apparatus is present in his histories: facts, citations, and footnotes, with references by chapter and verse to his sources. Maurois became an indefatigable and meticulous sifter of facts, a peruser of dusty documents, and a stern weigher of probabilities.

His own remark to the effect that he wished to introduce his compatriots to the English people is true as far as it goes, but it hardly goes far enough. Within this purpose, the reader asks whether he had auxiliary goals. Surely he had no wish to produce merely another long and scholarly account of the emergence of modern England from the centuries of strife and warfare with France. Nor could he as an amateur historian and a Frenchman hope to improve very much on the work of Green, Trevelyan, and the scores of other able and conscientious men, Englishmen and foreigners, who had gone before him. All of them had weighed, counted, tested, speculated and written about the facts which, when summarized, become a history of the British nation. Their books were available, many of them in French translation. What, then? What Maurois wished most of all to do was to produce an English history written for his compatriots, whose virtue would lie precisely in the fact that it was not produced by a professional historian for historians. He wished to demonstrate to the average reader, who seldom read history, what the events of British history, which they had studied in school books written from the French point of view, really looked like in Britain. He felt this had never been done before. Without bowing to nationalistic prejudices, he wanted to take a fresh look at Franco-British differences and rivalries. To achieve this, he has provided throughout his text constant cross references to events occurring simultaneously in the two countries. He makes the fairly safe assumption that his French readers are familiar with the history of their own country, and when he makes an analogical reference to events occurring simultaneously on both sides of the Channel, he assumes that there will be no need to provide a frame of reference. To explain events in Britain, he also indulged, perhaps somewhat too often, in the device of imagining what might have happened in France if English circumstances had been repeated there. He says, for instance, "Now imagine what our country would have been like if instead of Richelieu we had had a Cromwell."

Undoubtedly the best feature of Maurois' history of England is his success in remaining above the battle, for despite the comradeship and common victory of World War I, the Frenchman of the 1930's was not especially pro-British. Thus Maurois had to free himself of both conscious and unconscious nationalism when writing about a nation with which his own had been at war for centuries, indulging throughout recorded history in all the hostile acts against France that diplomacy, war, and intrigue could devise. Yet, in Maurois' pages, France is never upheld as a model for what Britain should have done, nor is England decried as a bad example, the ever-perfidious Albion. In his history he will not have France exalted nor England debased. He strives for and achieves a balance of impartiality between the two countries, and he deserves high praise for having applied to historical writing the dictum of Voltaire: "Seek neither to ridicule nor to condemn, seek only to understand."

The period of the Middle Ages in Britain is well narrated. This is a story which, with slight variations, can be told of all the countries of Western Europe. The omnipresence of the Catholic Church and its hierarchy, the struggle against the infidel, the rise of the merchant class, the eventual downfall of feudalism, and the rise of the towns and the bourgeoisie are phenomena to be found no less in France than in Britain and other areas of the continent. The story is a familiar one. It is with the emergence of the modern period, when English history becomes for all practical purposes the story of religious factionalism and intolerance, that Maurois' skill and maturity as an historian become apparent. He handles the rival sects and their noisy claims with dexterity and understanding. He quite forgets, as the true historian should, that he is a Jew, or a Frenchman, or a cosmopolitan practicing tolerance and patience. He tries rather to put himself successively in the place of the Quaker, the Catholic, the Puritan, and the dissenter, and he does this so well that if his reading about religious conflicts made him feel impatient with sectarianism or with the hairsplitting and intolerance of those about whom he was writing, he managed to disguise the fact completely.

The seventeenth century, as Maurois writes about it, makes intelligible the reasons for the bitter sectarian atmosphere that has characterized English history. In some of his pages he gives the period the kind of epic treatment achieved by Shakespeare in his historical plays. The reason, apparently, for this epic sweep is that Maurois, unlike many historians, is fascinated rather than bored by the religious problems of the age. Without taking sides between Cavaliers and Roundheads, he shows how the errors and fanaticism of both factions led to the political and social chaos of the period. He is delighted with the interplay of opposing forces which led to England's bloodless revolution, for in this he rightly sees the events which led in the long run to a stable democracy, yet quite without the bloodletting that was destined to occur before the same result could be achieved in France.

The reviewer of the *New York Times* praises him for this insight. He writes:

It is a supreme excellence of this book that M. Maurois recognized a factor which historians are apt to ignore. That factor is faith, and particularly a faith nourished on the English Bible. It is impossible to account for the careers of men like Gladstone, Salisbury, Baldwin and King George V if this factor be ignored. M. Maurois has not overstressed the religion of Britain. But he has insisted on seeing what has transformed Britain from the parts into a whole.[41]

On all occasions Maurois is at some pains to point out to his French readership the many instances where English history impinges on French. By so doing he provides a frame of reference for his countrymen, but he never shifts from his neutral position or forgets for a moment that he is writing English history. He writes at all times from an historian's point of view.

The panorama of eighteenth- and nineteenth-century colonial expansion, as the nations of Western Europe sought to change the post-Columbian period of discovery into one of empire building, is equally well described. If anything, Maurois may be accused of favoring the English cause, for he looks sympathetically upon their colonization of the New World and contrasts it favorably with the parallel efforts of the Spanish, the Portuguese, and those of his own country. He relates in some detail the military campaigns that led to the acquisition of Canada and India and the loss of the American colonies, but he does not overemphasize the military aspect of history. As a former woolen mill executive, Maurois follows the rise of mercantilism with obvious delight, for in its beginnings he imagines the struggles of his own ancestors as they worked to bring modern times into being. Quite apparent is his own competence in the field of economics. He writes of economic theory and practice with distinction and authority, a feat that cannot be always matched by the professional historians.

The first edition of *Histoire d'Angleterre,* written as it was in 1937, came to a close with the period between world wars. In the version that Maurois published in his collective works he brings events down to World War II. In both instances his conclusion seems hurried and unfinished. Fortunately in the most recent edition, that of 1963, the events of the twentieth century are given more space and more detailed treatment. Most readers will be grateful for this, for there are critics and historians who believe that Maurois is at his best when writing about his own time.

Everything considered, Maurois' *Histoire d'Angleterre* is an admirable work, a worthy début for one who had never written a history before. It is painstaking, scholarly, and authentic. Even a fairly minute comparison with the standard histories reveals no startling discrepancies in either fact or interpretation. This was no accident, for as he prepared to write this first history, Maurois took careful note of the technique of the historians whose works he was reading. When he began to write, he spared no pains to be accurate. His list of sources is impressive and omits few really important works or documents. His quotations from his sources likewise reveal that he used them well. At the same time it must be said that the history which he produced is distinctly Maurois in flavor. It has his engaging style, his narrative skill, and his faultless instinct for choosing out of many only those anecdotes and dramatic encounters that make a good history so much less dull than a bad one. History is, for Maurois, a story studied and observed in depth. Much of it is an account of the interaction of the noble and ignoble personalities of the many who strive against one another. In his view, a new history must not only reexamine well known sources but, if possible, must seek out and appraise new ones if a contribution to historical writing is to be made. Maurois did this in literary criticism in the book on Proust. Only occasionally did he break new ground in his histories. Except for this fact he might have won the highest accolade.

II A *History* of Amica *America*

The second of Maurois' major historical works was his *Histoire des Etats-Unis,* published in 1947, just ten years after the appearance of the *Histoire d'Angleterre.* In his introduction to this new history he says that the favorable reception accorded by the public to his history of England had led friends to suggest that he write a history of the United States, and after reflexion he decided to undertake the task. His stay in the United States during World War II afforded him both the time and the bibliographical resources that he needed, and so he was able to complete his work in good time.

The American who reads this book of history will find few surprises in it. But neither will he find much to complain about. Beginning with North American prehistory, and including meso-America, our author provides a carefully documented account of the age of exploration and the beginnings of recorded European settlements on the continent. As in his first history, Maurois strove to adhere to a strictly chronological order whenever possible. He presents the conflicting claims and achievements of the Dutch, French, English, Swedish, and Spanish colonists in that part of America which is now the United States. He traces the origin of the rivalries and quarrels that arose not only among the various nationalities, but among the several English groups of colonists. This is in many ways the best section of the book. By studying the England of the same period, he had become familiar with the conflicting views of the several religious sects that dominated the thinking of the Englishmen of the period, and so he was well prepared to understand and to interpret those quarrels as they were reflected among the transplanted Englishmen of the New World.

Maurois was also imbued with an adequate sense of the size of the task that confronted the founders of civilization in America, and he tries to communicate to his compatriots a sense of the grandeur of a pioneering venture in which all Europeans, whether personally involved or not, could rightfully take pride. The conquest of the wilderness is no mere phrase for him, and he tries to make his reader's heart beat faster as he describes the hardships, the dangers and the achievements of the pioneers. He creates the illusion that his own emotions are involved. He felt that he had to convey a sense of epic achievement, since most Europeans, however well acquainted with the geography of their school books, are seldom prepared to encounter the vastness of the American continent. Americans, on the other hand, take it for granted. Maurois already knew the North American continent well through his travels, and remembering his own first impressions, he was able to put into his history some of the wonder and awe which the pioneers must have felt as the extent of the land became known to them.

In retelling the slow but inevitable rise of the quarrel between Mother England and her American colonies, Maurois outdid himself. He had read widely in the period and already knew the point of view of the leading English statesmen of that period. He not only understood what was at stake, but was able to explain in detail how the conflicting emotions on both sides rose as the quarrel thickened and deepened. He communicates to his readers the views of the British Parliament. He presents the views of the handful of liberals in its midst who understood better than the others what was happening and who sought to postpone the inevitable. He depicts sympathetically the views of the colonists, torn between the desire to maintain their ties with the country they still called home (even though many of them were second, third or even fourth generation Americans) and their English love of justice which made it impossible for them to suffer injustice willingly. He makes his reader see that both Parliament and colonists, though they were but dimly aware of it, were facing an altogether new phenomenon: the relation of a new country, on new soil, with its parent body. This was something that had not happened in Europe since the fusion of the bar-

barians with the native population in those parts of the Roman Empire which they overran. When the colonial period ended and the war was concluded between Britain and the new United States, Maurois chronicles with obvious satisfaction the efforts of the new nation to govern itself, noting its self-consciousness as it assumed a role that might well influence the history of other nations in the years to come.

Perhaps because his American readers knew that Maurois was also a biographer, they were perhaps overly anxious to find portraits of famous Americans in his history. Of course, they are to be found at every turn. As deftly as in a pencil sketch, Maurois pictures the young Washington, the British general Braddock, Benjamin Franklin, and all others whom he must mention as his narrative unfolds. But he never yields to the temptation to forget to write history in order to write biography instead. His aim, successfully achieved, is to place his skill as a biographer in the hands of the historian, and his intelligent use of that skill to highlight and interpret history is one of his best claims to serious attention as an historian.

After concluding his account of the stirring days of the Revolutionary War and the era of factional and regional strife that preceded and followed it, Maurois found himself confronted with the era of John Quincy Adams and his successors, a period that even Americans are prone to find dull and devoid of highlights. It is an era as slow and tiresome as the previous one was stirring, and, except for the brief appearance on the scene of Andrew Jackson, it must be accounted a history reader's bugbear. Undaunted by the prospect, Maurois plunged into his story. The period had, after all, a challenge for him by reason of its total unfamiliarity. The result was a series of unforgettable vignettes of the pygmies and half-giants who strove against each other for power and recognition.

With the arrival on the scene of Abraham Lincoln, prime material is available again, but though he was undoubtedly impressed by the importance of Lincoln, Maurois did not yield to the temptation to write the history of the Civil War in terms of Lincoln and his greatness alone. He chose rather to weave Lincoln's life into the larger framework of the sectional conflict and to deal with its international as well as its national implications. Above all, he kept his perspective, and the reader's attention is focused on the war as a whole. His understanding of the period is solidly based in wide reading and much reflexion. He depicts feelingly the coming of the war and the conflicting loyalties that were involved. He shows the heart-rending nature of the decision which led Lee and others to abjure their allegiance to the Union. He pictures well the beginning of the conflict with its change of generals, as McClellan was replaced by Meade, and Meade by Grant, leading inexorably to Appomatox and the defeat of the South. He shows comprehension of the military campaigns of the war and makes them come alive with both narrative and descriptive skills. At the same time he does not allow his readers to forget the social and political aspects of the struggle, such as the plight of the freed slaves and the destruction of the South's economy, to mention but two. Certainly the French reader, coming to grips for the first time with a detailed account of the Civil War period, should be not only enlightened but sympathetic.

Continuing with the period of President Andrew Johnson, Maurois' interpretive skill is no less well employed. He deals ably with the reconstruction and carpet-bag era and speaks frankly, assigning praise and blame where he believes they belong.

If a letdown occurs, it is in the treatment of the following period which, after all, resembles the age of John Quincy Adams and John Tyler. To say this is no criticism of Maurois, for one frequently detects a similar defect in the writings of American historians when they deal with the same period. The fact is that the beginning of the get-rich-quick era, with its rapid industrialization, its quarrels between management and labor, and its preoccupation with the gold and silver standard, cuts but a sorry figure in contrast with the period of the Civil War and its immediate aftermath. Tilden and Bryan and their like resemble the half-heroes of the age of Tyler, and all the objectivity and sympathy in the world cannot render either the period or its leading figures really exciting.

From this point to the turn of the century, Maurois appears to admit by implication that there is truly only one bright spot, that furnished by the quicksilvery, inconsistent, and exuberant Theodore Roosevelt. The biographer in Maurois treats the president with the detached amusement and sympathy he so richly deserves. Roosevelt, the idealist in home affairs, the blatantly cynical in foreign, the would-be intellectual who wrote histories and treatises on history and who at the same time fancied himself a cowpuncher and pioneer, is served up with gusto. We are shown Teddy campaigning for Civil Service reform, trying to govern decently according to Christian principles while at the same time he brutally snatches away a slice of Colombia for his canal. All these events our historian records not only faithfully but with humor and understanding.

The period of World War I is treated with an unexpected objectivity when we remember that Maurois was himself a participant and a Frenchman. American aid to France is also seen in its proper perspective. As usual, he assumes the posture of an impartial bystander. When he does take sides, it is because he is endeavoring to present America's dilemma and her decision to participate as seen through the eyes of Woodrow Wilson and the millions of Americans who wanted to have nothing to do with European quarrels. He depicts, too, the attitude of the many Americans who regarded all European nations as equally decadent, with the possible exception of Germany whose "energy" they admired. Wilson's role, while not unduly emphasized, is given ample space, and we are not surprised that Maurois, during his first visit to Princeton, was collecting material for a biography of the president. Unfortunately, he never wrote it. Wilson's part in founding the ill-fated League of Nations is described in detail, as is the final illness which took him out of the struggle.

In the first edition of *Histoire des Etats-Unis*, the post-war period, from Calvin Coolidge to the beginnings of World War II, is condensed into a very few pages. Its concluding remarks are thereby made to appear as if hastily written. This defect was rectified in a second edition, published in 1959. In the latter volume the period between the two wars, with the depression, the presidency of Franklin D. Roosevelt, and its domestic and international problems, is handled competently and understandingly. The book was favorably reviewed by Maurois' fellow academician Jules Romains in *Les Nouvelles littéraires*,[42] and the reviewer, a fellow exile during the war years, had more than a little competence to judge it. His conclusion was that it is clear and thoughtful, avoiding both partiality and superficiality. His one complaint, which he adds almost apologetically, is that Maurois kept his book, if anything, on too even a keel. "It seems to me that the relief is not always sharply drawn," said Romains, but his conclusion was that Maurois' history was a useful one for contemporary Frenchmen. America, the world power, must be known and understood by the rest of the world. Still Maurois was not quite satisfied that he had rounded off the story exactly as he had wished.

His desire to continue his history down to the present was gratified by an ingenious project to be called *Histoire parallèle*. Louis Aragon, the well-known Communist sympathizer, was asked to undertake a contemporary history of Soviet Russia while Maurois would write the contemporary history of the United States. Thus the period that had a lame conclusion in Maurois' original history was to be given the full treatment in two volumes. If any doubt about Maurois' skill as a historian still existed, and this is difficult to see, this history was to dispel it. His work is an accurate and brilliant account of the presidencies of Wilson, Coolidge, Harding, Hoover, Roosevelt, Truman, Eisenhower, and Kennedy. The task was in some ways more formidable than anything he had previously attempted, for, as contemporary historians discover to their chagrin, ours is an age of excessively complete documentation. No statesman or politician throws away so much as a laundry list, and it becomes the historian's task to winnow his material thoroughly in order to discard the ninety percent that is trivial and find and use the remainder that is indispensable. This Maurois did, far better, be it said, than his colleague who was trying to do a similar task for the USSR.

Both histories are followed by a complementary volume in which the authors report on interviews with national leaders in a variety of fields. Maurois talked with some thirty-five persons: Bernstein for music; Galbraith for economics; Conant for education, as examples. The interviews that he recorded are characterized by their thoughtfulness and candor, but it should be added that the questions that Maurois asked were extremely skillful. He wished to elicit responses that would reveal American thought and American hopes within the realistic framework of our time. He avoided politics in this instance almost entirely. The contrast with what Aragon was able to accomplish in the USSR is striking. Whereas the Americans are frank about their country's faults and her unsolved problems, the Russians who were interviewed fall back almost to a man on the clichés of the party, so that the seeker after the truth about Russia will have to look elsewhere for his information. These books are large and copiously illustrated, and the carefully chosen photographs tell much about both America and the USSR.

As a kind of footnote to his interest in the contemporary scene, Maurois wrote a penetrating introduction to André Brisson's *Les Américains de Kennedy*. Therein he not only pays tribute to but analyzes the achievements of the late president, of whom he was an outspoken admirer.

III *More History*

If the two long, solid, and carefully researched histories of the Anglo-Saxon democracies were a kind of *tour de force* for a French writer who began as a novice in historical writing, then to compose a history of his own country should have been a labor of love solidly based on the experience acquired in the earlier ventures. For such an undertaking, Maurois had been prepared by patriotism, education, and a lifetime of living within her borders. His work appeared in 1947. He begins, as it his custom, with the prehistoric peoples who inhabited the land of France, and he brings his readers by steps through the Middle Ages, the Renaissance, the Wars of Religion, and the reigns of the successive Louis down to the Revolution. He dwells fondly on the nineteenth century which he knows so well with its colonialism, its rivalry with Great Britain, its quarrels with Germany, and finally he comes down to modern times. The facts are all there. Yet something is lacking. The vignettes of Charlemagne, Saint Louis, Jeanne d'Arc, Francis I, and Voltaire lack the sharp outlines we expect of Maurois. Above all, they supply little of that biographical spark which so enlivened his pages in previous histories. He appears to have hurried this history, a suggestion made probable by the fact that in this volume, as in neither of those preceding it, he makes use of whole pages of the works of other historians. It is as if he had found out that what he was about to say had already been said, and well said, by someone else, so that when this occurs, he lets the others take over. To do so is bad history writing and suggests at the very least that if what he has to tell has already been much better said, then there is little reason for writing another history.

There is, in fact, reason to wonder just what Maurois' actual purpose was. He says in his preface that a friend suggested that he complete his duo by making it a trilogy to contain the histories of the three great modern democracies. The suggestion may have come at a bad time, perhaps when he had a more than usually large number of projects under way. Whatever the reason, Maurois does not appear to have put his heart into his work. And if he wrote it merely to cap the other two, this fact, too, detracts from its effect. Of course, Maurois is never without his better moments. His writing is lively for the most part, and it is dotted here and there with apt quotations and bright anecdotes. These he had used more sparingly in his other histories.

The phenomenon of Maurois' relative failure in his *Histoire de France* is a curious one. After he had weathered the dullness of sectarian politics and the lackluster periods of the history of America, he seemed to lose his footing in such exciting periods of French history as the seventeenth century, which comes from his pen without life-giving enthusiasm. Homer nods, so the saying goes; Maurois does likewise in this book.

In 1965 Maurois published his *Histoire d'Allemagne*. Of its 295 pages more than half are illustrations. The actual history is thereby reduced to a rather small compass, and it suffers thereby. Without skimping, it was scarcely possible to treat so large a subject in so few pages. Still the account is clear and readable and has the usual virtue of impartiality. When, on one occasion, Maurois strays from the path of historical neutrality, it is to castigate the Communist regime of East Germany for repressive measures which he considers absurd.

Fairly early in his career, Maurois wrote a book which has been difficult to assign a place in his work. Some consider *Edouard VII et son temps* (1933) a history, others, a biography. Maurois himself appears to count it as history, for he says in his preface to it in the collected works, "It is not a biography, but the tableau of a period, and a gallery of portraits." [43] Certainly it is not the usual sort of biography. Everything considered it is more of a history *cum* biography than a biography *cum* history. The writing of this book was undertaken with obvious delight, for it gave its author the kind of situation that he liked: a historical era and an important human figure to participate in and to influence its events. From first to last, Edward is the focal point for a narrative that encompasses not only the British court and the British nation, but also (because of the complexity of British foreign relations) most of the rest of the world as well. Thus, all that happens touches Edward if only tangentially.

Both as Prince of Wales and as King, Edward emerges from this book as a very human and engaging man. He was also, a fact often overlooked, a competent statesman who used the limited powers granted him by the British constitution to their fullest extent. In this he was so successful that Maurois is able to say that at the time of Edward's death the British monarchy was even stronger than it had been during the reign of his mother, Queen Victoria. The book is rich in vignettes. The picture of the German Kaiser and the German, French, and other statesmen who are seen in their dealings with Edward are well painted. The French are, if anything, slightly less appealing than the British, for our historian went to great lengths to avoid the accusation of a patriotic bias.

The wars and rumors of wars, the foreign and domestic policies of Britain and of the continent that occupied the front pages of the newspapers for so many years, all seem tame in retrospect, but Maurois' account of them is never dull, and he maintains throughout a ring of authenticity which is the surest proof of careful research and writing.

No one can read this account of late nineteenth-century Britain without sharing Maurois' respect for her monarchy as a political institution. His admiration for Britain extends also to the British character. Unlike many Frenchmen, he has come to the realization that Britain's famed "Anglo Saxon hypocrisy" is not really hypocrisy at all, and that if Britain appears to act from moralistic motives well mixed with self-interest, she is little different in this respect from other countries, since all nations are prone to rationalize the national need as a moral imperative. But if Britain is little different in this from any other nation, Maurois nonetheless credits her intentions with being relatively decent in a way that other nations might well learn to imitate. *Edouard VII* is a long book and its details are many, but Maurois maintains an admirable balance between biography and history. The reader comes to know Edward well, but the man will always be inseparable from the times in which his biographer-historian has placed him.

IV *Current History*

Among Maurois' publications are several other books which may be loosely classified as historical in nature. The first of these was *Tragédie en France* (1940), an account of the overrunning of France by the Nazis, a spectacle to which Maurois as a demobilized veteran of the so-called phony war was an eye witness and of which he and his wife were a part. At the time of his landing in America two facts were uppermost in Maurois' mind: the miracle of his own escape and the obvious and overwhelming nature of the American disillusionment with France. This point of view reflected itself in newspapers and magazines, on the radio, and in private conversations. Americans had been taught by French propaganda to believe the Maginot Line impregnable and a kind of sea wall that would keep the Germans away from the Atlantic and prevent them from attacking the United States. The fact that planes had flown over the French defenses and that tanks had outflanked it were dismissed as details. Faith in the line was gone and, with it, faith in France. Maurois found this state of affairs intolerable and he went into action to try to change it. In speeches, articles, and pronouncements on the radio he tried to present the facts as he saw them, but he felt that his efforts were not reaching a large enough public. He decided that what was needed was a clear, straightforward, and reasoned account of what had happened, and this he set out to write.

In approaching the American public, Maurois was wise enough to realize two things: first, that his effort would be worse than no effort at all if he withheld the facts and tried to gloss over French failures and shortcomings; and second, that he must remain unemotional and write as a candid observer. He succeeded in both endeavors. First he explained in detail why the French labor unions, torn between the ideologies of socialism and communism, were unwilling to go all out for war production. He described as concretely as he could the venality of certain French politicians, greedy in peace and unable or unwilling to change their ways even with the enemy staring them in the face. He analyzed the opposition to the Republic among certain rightist groups who proclaimed loudly and idiotically "better Hitler than the Jew Blum." He discussed the superannuated generals with their mentality of "safety behind impenetrable defenses." He dealt with the obsolete planning of the general staff and with the general dislike of war from which the French recoiled instinctively as they recalled the wars of 1870 and 1914. Then he demonstrated that facing this planned and unplanned chaos was the German army, new in weapons and strategy, high in morale and in hatred of France, and ready to unleash a new and terrible kind of warfare which would dwarf all previous conflicts between the two countries.

The plea was well put and had the merit of historical accuracy as well as frankness. It also made full use of Maurois' skill as a capsule biographer. There were intimate sketches of General Giraud and other French leaders and a picture of Winston Churchill as he began his wartime task. Life among the troops manning the Maginot Line was portrayed. Above all, he showed how the Germans used the period of apparent stalemate to their own advantage, letting the French and British grow tired of the war and lose their will to fight. The book was a combination of good historical writing and good public relations. It concluded with the firm yet not sentimental conviction that France would be reborn from the ruins and that the kind of values that National Socialism stood for were bound to go down in the end. He expressed the hope that once the conflict had been resolved, the wartime allies would have the good sense never to be parted again. It may be urged, and it is true, that this conclusion, however well meant or necessary, turns the book from a history into a pamphlet. But in the body of the work Maurois does not mix the two aspects of his task. The history is straightforward with no nonsense, and his plea for France and the post-war world at the end is a kind of epilogue.

Among the critics were inevitable dissenters from the generally favorable reaction. G. M. A. Grube, the reviewer of the *Canadian Forum,* made this objection:

He does not see historical forces very clearly in the political field, and in the economic field he shows no trace of seeing them at all. Hence, while he helps us to discover how things happened, he cannot tell us why they happened, and he travels somewhat on the surface of things, a surface, however, which is still of absorbing interest.[44]

Maurois had no illusion that his explanation of why France fell would convince or satisfy everyone, and so he continued to accept and even invite opportunities to speak to audiences about France. He insisted in his speeches that France would ultimately throw off the Nazi yoke and return to her position as a leading democracy. He also wrote newspaper and magazine articles to the same effect. He thought enough of three of these to publish them as a book under the title *Espoirs et souvenirs* (1943). In the first chapter he recalls nostalgically the old Paris "which looked so bright and gay," and continues with an exhortation to French prisoners of war not to lose hope or their faith in France. In the time to come, their country will need all her sons to help rebuild her martyred cities. Much of this is polemic and patriotic writing merely on the fringe of history, but Maurois was too good an historian not to try to make history himself by seeking to influence men's minds.

Also in the nature of pamphlets were two other commentaries on the post-war period. The first was but two pages in length, the other was of book length, but their purpose was identical: to exhort Frenchmen regarding the present and future of their country. In the first he joined with Louis de Broglie, Albert Caquet, and Georges Duhamel to write a booklet entitled *Problèmes d'aujourd'hui* (1952). In its pages each author exhorted his country to seek greatness, and each assumed the role of chiding moralist. Maurois preached that what his country needed was a judicious combination of Christian charity, the Graeco-Roman concept of liberty, and an intelligent application of the scientific method. Four years later, in the book-length discussion entitled *La France change de visage* (1956), he was led to further pronouncements regarding the nature of his country's problems and to give advice as to how they should be handled. This again was scarcely history; it was the sort of thing in which the historian sometimes finds himself engaged when he is the target of reporters who expect him to foretell the future as well as describe the past. As the title implies, the book is a survey of the changes in France since World War II and an estimate of the probable direction to the future. Maurois then offers advice regarding measures to meet the probable needs in all areas. He believes that education, for instance, will need basic reform in order to educate more children. Commerce, agriculture, and nationally sponsored research must assume new responsibilities. Further, as an unashamed moralist, he urges upon his countrymen once again certain virtues and values which will enable them better to cope with the future. These values are, by and large, the traditional ones: hard work, humility, patience, and patriotism. There was little here that had not already been expressed in his earlier two-page essay.

Also germane to the consideration of Maurois as a historian is a brief satire in which he imagines what might have happened if certain events had not occurred as they did. To amuse himself with such a speculation, he wrote back in 1931 a short piece entitled *Si le roi Louis XVI avait eu un grain de fermeté* ("If King Louis XVI had had an ounce of firmness"). In this little fantasy he imagines that Turgot, the dismissed prime minister, was recalled. History would then have been changed. France would have begun to prosper. There would have been no aid from France to the American colonies in their war for independence, no French Revolution, and no Napoleon. France would have set up a constitutional monarchy on the English model, and the political alignment of the modern world would be quite different from what it is. Inconsequential, even as imaginary history, this little sketch is illustrative of Maurois' biographical conception of history. It amused him to imagine that if Turgot had been in charge at a crucial moment the mob would not have gotten out of hand, etc., etc. The imaginary history concludes with a brief fantasy in which an historian in heaven discovers that in the celestial kingdom two sets of records are kept: one of events as they have actually occurred, and one of events as they might have been. Such romantic fooling is, of course, anathema to many professional historians, but, as an amateur, Maurois allows himself the luxury of poking fun at himself and at history itself.

The ensemble of Maurois' historical writing is considerable in bulk, running to thousands of pages. Judged by the sheer size of his readership, he was one of the most important historians of the century. Nor is it possible to ascribe his popularity solely to the success of his work in other fields. His style and manner of presentation were probably decisive factors in his success. An outstanding quality also was his flawless sense of perspective, that mysterious quality that is always attributed to a talented historian and denied to a poor one. With perspective the historian can write of the past while he prepares readers for the future. At the same time he has to avoid references to things to come thereby implying foolishly that he has gifts of prophecy. Maurois had this ability in high degree. He also had perspective regarding the international scene. He was able, without apparent effort, to lay aside the nationalistic assumptions that make so many histories unpalatable outside the countries in which they are written. Not only was he never guilty of the petty crime of narrowness in his attitude toward historical events, but he had the positive virtue of writing for a French audience, as a Frenchman, without ever seeming to be bounded by the borders of France. When, as he frequently did, he referred his putative French reader to events occurring simultaneously in the rest of Europe, he did so accurately and without prejudice.

It may also be said without fear of contradiction that Maurois, like every respectable historian since Voltaire, aspired to be a social and cultural historian to whom politics, whether in peace or in war, was but one phase of national life. To avoid the temptation that besets every historian to overemphasize political factors, he was at some pains to inform himself regarding religion, commerce, invention, and science. He studied the books of the social critics, reformers, reactionaries, prophets, and pundits of each epoch and each nation that he had under consideration. In America he had to come to grips with the anti-slavery movement, with reconstruction, populism, muck-raking and anti-intellectualism. Writing of England, he had on his hands the complex problem of an economic, political, and social order that was divided among religious sects, and whose evolution was frequently determined by the outcome of sectarian battles. In France he had to deal not only with the nation's position in Europe, but with the complicated question of her involvement on other continents. And these were but a few of the complex issues that, as a historian of all three nations, he had to take into account and to handle competently.

Arts and letters also had to be assigned their proper role, and for this task Maurois had the good fortune to have read widely not only in French and European literature, but in American and English literature as well. The arts he knew less well, but he studied them for his purpose, and his accounts of artistic endeavors are not hastily contrived as frequently occurs in some historical writing.

In the field of political writing, Maurois shows considerable skill in unraveling the tangled skeins of conflicting national wills and the men behind them. The political framework also, though it was not allowed to dominate, had to assume its rightful place in history, and this it did. Why, then, was he content to get his facts principally from other historians? In his biographies he was not content to reuse well-known material. He read, in addition to all existing biographies of his subjects their personal letters and all the other original documents that he could find. In his writing of history he seldom did so. A possible answer may be found in his modesty and in a realistic appraisal of the difficulty of his task. He was aware that in some cases professional historians spend a lifetime of study and research merely to become acquainted with a single aspect of the life of a single nation. He knew from experience that his full time was required over a period of years simply to become acquainted with the documentation regarding a single person, and he realized that it would be impossible for him, unless he wished to give up all other activities, to become an expert in the historical background of a single period of a single nation. He saw that even the vast documentation available for a life of George Sand was puny compared to that obtainable for the study of a single year of the French Revolution. Disliking to cast a cursory glance at the documents, as a mere pretense that he had studied them, he chose the more honest course of declaring that his histories would be a new presentation of existing material. For his pains he had the word "popularizer" thrown at him accusingly, frequently with the envy of the professional who must have wished that his pen were as facile as that of this gifted amateur. Maurois, meanwhile, has never made any protest to the critics for their estimate of his historical work, which, in general, was fairly and sensibly reviewed for what it was. Popularization was after all what he aimed at. He wanted to encourage people to read history. He thought that by so doing they might rid themselves of the prejudices of ignorance. He wished to see the public informed, and if this was his goal, he succeeded admirably. His histories have been the favorites of the reading public of two continents.

CHAPTER 5

The Writer Turned Critic

ANDRÉ Maurois did not set out to be a literary critic. During his years in the lycée his fondness for literary analysis made him think that he would like to be a writer rather than evaluate the writings of others. The role of critic was, in a sense, thrust upon him, but its importance in his life and work gradually increased. As we have seen, so distinguished a biographer would inevitably be asked to discuss the art of biography in a lecture series. Equally inevitably, as his novels increased in numbers and popularity, he would be asked questions about his methods of writing and even his opinions about the writing of others. But his willingness to yield to such importunities meant more than that he was simply asked to do so. The case of Roger Martin du Gard is well known. He has been asked repeatedly to discuss his methods and to evaluate his own work. He has always stubbornly refused. Thornton Wilder in the United States has been equally reticent. Both of these men, the Frenchman and the American, believe that an author should write rather than talk about writing. Others, like Georges Duhamel, appear to enjoy the public analysis of their own techniques. Maurois belongs among the latter group, and talking about one's own work is but a step removed from talking about the work of others, past and present, and a discussion of literature in general.

In Maurois' case the opportunity for speaking and writing about literature and its techniques was provided by the universities. After an invitation from Cambridge to lecture on biography, Maurois received invitations successively from Princeton, and Columbia to occupy lectureships on their faculty. During his World War II exile in the United States, American colleges and universities vied with each other for his services, and his appearances in the classroom and on the lecture platform were greatly multiplied. During this period he received and accepted invitations for a resident lectureship from the University of Kansas City and from Mills College. Whenever he appeared before students, he talked about some aspect of French literature, and the lectures which resulted compose a body of literary criticism respectable in quantity though somewhat uneven in quality. Later on, his cordial relations with the publishers and editors of both continents led to his writing prefaces for new editions of the great books or introductions to new books. Finally, his marriage to the niece of Marcel Proust, to whom he had already devoted several articles, led to a critical study of the man and his work. Thus Maurois' acceptance of the role of literary critic was mainly accidental.

I *The Biographer as a Critic*

We have already seen that Maurois approached the art of biography seriously both as lecturer and practitioner. He read voluminously on the subject. When he praised Lytton Strachey, it was after he had read his work and knew it intimately. Wide reading had always been Maurois' way of becoming acquainted with a subject. In and of itself, his work as a biographer also led Maurois to interest himself in the evaluation of literature. In order to write of Byron, George Sand, Hugo, Balzac, and even Disraeli, Maurois had to analyze in detail the literary achievements of each subject. Nor would a man of Maurois' literary acumen have been willing to accept the judgments of others. He therefore had to read in depth the productions of his subjects, and he was led thereby to such value judgments as appear in all the biographies. In general, it may be said of his literary evaluations that they do not differ widely from those generally held, though he frequently disagrees in some detail with the accepted critical view. But in all cases his opinions are clearly and succinctly expressed. On occasion they are even expressed in memorable form. Here, for instance, is his conclusion regarding the *Mémoires d'outre-tombe* of Chateaubriand:

He wrote only for others and lived only for himself, said Joubert at the time of *Le Génie*. By the time of the *Mémoires* he had reached the point of writing mainly for himself. Despairing of understanding himself he had remade himself. Of the strange dreams and incoherent acts which are the stuff of existence he had woven an admirable and coherent account. Passionately devoted to greatness he gave his childhood in his book a terrible and superb Combourg. For lord of the manner a Shakespearian old man. For the companion of his old age a Juliet who was more sylph than woman. Because by the power of his genius he had

linked his fragile existence to the sublime drama of Christianity and to
the epic of the French nation, he had become in his own eyes a dramatic
and epic personage. It is the triumph of his art to have conquered nature
himself.[45]

The space allotted to literary criticism in the biographies increased
as time went on. In *Ariel* the treatment of Shelley's poetry had been
cavalier and almost incidental, an omission pounced upon by the
critics. According to their view, the works of a poet, particularly
one so intensely personal as Shelley, are so intimately tied up with
his life that one cannot write intelligently of the one and omit the
other. In other words, a biography of Shelley that does not deal
seriously and at length with his poetry is *ipso facto* a bad biography.
The point may be debatable, but Maurois took the strictures to heart.
Beginning with *Byron,* he saw to it that each writer's life story was
interlarded with copious literary details and quotations from his
works. He also gave his estimate of the works in question. In *Byron*
the very conspicuousness of the incidental literary judgments makes
them appear somewhat ill-digested. Evidently Maurois was aware
of this, for his technique improved with time, and in *Hugo* and
Balzac the literary productions of the two writers are discussed and
evaluated in such a proper proportion to the biographical details as
to form a coherent and balanced whole. Literary history and literary
criticism thus assume their rightful place as an important but by
no means proponderant aspect of the life story of an author.

The early lectures on Charles Dickens (1935) are an example of
Maurois' ambivalent attitude at a time when he had not yet solved
the problem to his satisfaction. On the basis of the contents of the
lectures, it was his intention to talk principally about Dickens as a
novelist. But Dickens the fatuous self-hero could hardly be left out
of consideration. So much of what Dickens wrote can be explained
by what he was that to talk about his work with but scant reference
to his life appeared impossible. The result was a literary essay which
evaluated the novels while it permitted the hearer or reader to catch
glimpses of the man who wrote them. The result was good, but,
unlike Maurois' maturer productions, this essay still reveals here
and there his struggles with his materials, and the not totally resolved
problem of how to mix biography and literary criticism in satisfactory
proportions.

The life of Turgenev posed a similiar problem. In appearance the
Russian novelist's life story is the subject of the lectures, but since

his relatively uneventful life lent itself but ill to full-length biographical treatment, a considerable amount of space had to be devoted to his literary work. Furthermore, Maurois cannot conceive of literary criticism without a modicum of the key-hole peeping into man's life that was so important a part of Sainte-Beuve's critical method. And while he once declared in a lecture that it is entirely possible to enjoy Homer without any working knowledge of his biography, still in our time a fuller and more adult appreciation of a man's work can be achieved when the biography is known. A knowledge of the personality, the struggles, the aspirations, in sum, the life story of an individual writer contributed notably to an understanding of his works. In fact, Maurois reports such knowledge as an indispensable ingredient in the sophisticated enjoyment of a work of art. For this reason, and additionally because he has come to think in terms of biography and cannot much help himself, Maurois never fails to provide biographical details when he sets out to describe and to evaluate the works of an author, whether of our time or of a past century.

We have already seen that Maurois the biographer was strongly attracted to a number of British authors, both of his own and of preceding generations, and that under the collective title *Magiciens et logiciens* he dealt briefly with a number of them. He thus describes the occasion for studying and writing about them:

These essays concerning some English writers of our times were written for the *Société des Conférences* and were the annual course of 1935. It was my purpose to choose writers who had brought to their generation not only esthetic pleasure but a philosophy. There were too many even of the latter for it to be possible to study them all.[46]

For his series he chose, as already noted, Kipling, Wells, Shaw, Chesterton, Conrad, Strachey, Mansfield, Lawrence, and Aldous Huxley. To give his French audience, presumably unfamiliar with even the names of most of these writers, an inkling of their identity, each was given brief but satisfactory biographical treatment. But biography was not Maurois' sole reason for speaking and writing about these persons. He had always been fond of sharing with the public his own tastes in reading with the hope that others might share his pleasure. The result is literary criticism of a genial sort. If he was seldom ready with reproach or reproof to the authors under consideration, he had the excuse, not available to him when speaking to university audiences, that the public preferred to hear about books that it would enjoy reading rather than to listen to scholarly analysis of the faults and virtues of the great books. Applying, therefore, a slightly different criterion to our judgment of Maurois' achievement, we can say of this series of lectures that he chose his authors well and treated them competently and pleasantly.

Rudyard Kipling, whose works Maurois had read as a boy, attracted him as a subject. Most of Kipling's imperial vision and his British propaganda admittedly escaped him at the time. What he did absorb from Kipling's books was a picture of exotic places and an emphasis on heroics, a combination of action and idealism. These traits he still admired as an adult, and he counted them among mankind's finest qualities. He further suggested that, nature imitating art, Britain's empire builders had been profoundly influenced by Kipling even to the point of trying to emulate the feats of his heroes while doing their duty to Queen and country. His last and highest praise for Kipling is that his effects were never faked. He wrote only of what he knew.

Joseph Conrad interested him for similar reasons. Like Kipling, he was mainly concerned with life as it was lived outside England. As a writer he was impressed by Conrad's competence in everything that he did, whether as a sea captain or as a writer. He finds Conrad, the Pole, in some ways more English than Kipling. The latter, he thinks, had a non-English streak of oriental mysticism in him while Conrad was strictly a no-nonsense student of character whether on the deck of a ship or on land. In fact, wherever man found it necessary to come to grips with basic impulses, Conrad liked to observe him. The literary criticism in this essay is excellent.

Maurois found in H. G. Wells a solid British character. Unlike most of the critics who tend to dismiss Wells as superficial, he believed that this self-educated man, was a great and original thinker and that his influence on his age was considerable. For though Wells was a pessimist, he not only tried to see the shape of things to come, but with remarkable prescience he sought to turn the world away from its doom. Maurois analyzed carefully the progress of Wells' thought from the Utopian to the didactic.

The article on George Bernard Shaw is more penetrating than most. One would not ordinarily expect a Frenchman to understand an Irishman who, without divesting himself of his Irishness, is still a very British author; yet Maurois does so. He also sympathizes wholeheartedly with Shaw's penchant for writing nonsense in order to have sense understood by his very exaggerations. He approved of Shaw's policy of insulting British politicians in the public interest. When he analyzed Shaw's plays, he demonstrated how the Irishman's irritating brand of social criticism made him a success in the society that he pretended to scorn. He understood, too, why such tactics made him a failure in France when his works were translated and sold there. As a tag to his published lecture, Maurois appended some remarks by Shaw in rebuttal of his own. As usual, Shaw feigned that he had been misunderstood. Altogether, this is one of Maurois' best critical essays.

Aldous Huxley, too, is an unconventional writer. At the time of Maurois' evaluation he had not yet done some of his best work. Maurois was evidently fascinated by him, particularly when he discovered that Huxley's patterns of thought were often directly opposed to his own. His evaluation calls attention to Huxley's faith in science and the consequent neglect in his works of the common man —the only man, according to Chesterton, whom Maurois admires, who matters at all. He finds in Huxley a militant skepticism toward the church that baffles and annoys him. One wonders why. Huxley's skepticism is not very different from the attitude frequently found among French intellectuals, and his faith in the power of the intellect is not very different from Maurois' own. Yet he appears to feel a decided antipathy toward Huxley.

Most readers and most critics took considerable pleasure in this book of sketches, but its American edition drew a blast which is typical of the unfriendly reviews his books have sometimes drawn. Writing in the *Nation*, R. P. Blackmur had this to say:

The lectures . . . are light and easy, pretentious and irritating, inconsistent and revealing. Addressed to a French and popular audience they say for the most part all the easy enthusiastic things that make a substitute for actual reading, and they take for granted nothing but the hard things that come only with slow knowledge and intimate attention.[47]

Such an attack, although unfair, raises a question that is crucial to Maurois and his work. By implication it asks the question whether the French public, which presumably knew little or nothing about the authors in question, would not have been just as well off without Maurois' essay. In a word, is superficial knowledge worth anything? For to assume that without Maurois the "public" would ever take the time for the kind of painstaking study that the reviewer advocates is to ask the impossible. Maurois' answer is to be found in his life work. He obviously neither despises the public nor does he expect too much of it, and so he has frequently contributed popular culture to its store of knowledge. Other reviews of this same book were quite different. Henry Seidel Canby, for instance, was obviously delighted with it.[48]

As already noted, *Destins exemplaires* (1952) was a similar volume. It was followed by a third volume of sketches, entitled *Robert et Elizabeth Browning, portraits suivis de quelques autres* (1955). In neither of these collections is literary criticism in the forefront. In both instances Maurois is far more interested in capsule biography than in literary criticism. Many of the writers presented are personal friends of his and, therefore, what he sets out to describe is a sympathetic personality. Still, inevitably, literary opinions are occasionally expressed in the course of his narratives. He was especially interested in the problems of young people, which is probably why he chose to include Katherine Mansfield and D. H. Lawrence in his group of essays. The former hated the bourgeois contentment of her middle-class family in New Zealand, and the stories she wrote were in part the product of her rebelliousness. The case of D. H. Lawrence is not dissimilar. The son of a coal miner, Lawrence hated the class from which he sprang, so that as a reverse snob he wished to move into the upper class. He succeeded to the extent that he managed to marry a German noblewoman, the former wife of an Englishman. She left everything, including happiness, to follow him all over the world. The writing of Lawrence, including his sexual protest, was seen by Maurois as his attempt to escape from himself. For these reasons, the writing of Katherine Mansfield is satirical, and that of Lawrence, as he seeks to escape from taboos, is shocking. Thus does biography explain literature.

II *The University Lecturer as a Critic*

The American university lectures that were subsequently published as *Etudes littéraires* (1947) are an excellent demonstration of Maurois' method as a critic. Each essay begins with a short biography of varying length. Sometimes a paragraph suffices; at other times he requires a full page or half a dozen pages. Then follows a discussion of the writer's outstanding works, analyzed topically with ample quotations to document the points that are made and to provide a sample of his style. For this series of lectures, which were published in two volumes, Maurois tells us that he invariably picked authors whom he liked, a warning, admittedly, to those who are disappointed at finding little or no adverse criticism of the books that he talks about. From preference he leans toward the novel. He gave his students Jules Romains, François Mauriac, Georges Duhamel, Antoine de Saint-Exupéry, André Gide, and Jacques de Lacretelle. Poetry gets less space, although he devotes a chapter each to Charles Péguy and Paul Claudel who, as he must have discovered, have little appeal for the average American undergraduate. He also included the philospher Bergson whose philosophy was not very congenial to audiences that had been raised, whether consciously or unconsciously, on William James' pragmatism. These lectures, even if we make allowance for editing after delivery, are witty and charming. They are also rather superficial, a fact not to be wondered at in view of the audience for which they were intended. Maurois obviously wished to entertain as well as to instruct, and though he pays tribute to the intelligence and perspicacity of his American students, he seldom ventured into deep water with them.

As Maurois tends to be a rationalist, albeit with intuitive leanings, one may speculate as to why in a small group of lectures, prepared for a non-French audience, he chose to include two poets whose work, although diverse in character, have many qualities in common. Péguy, like Claudel, was of humble origin. Like Claudel, he lost his faith early only to regain it and find in it the inspiration for his poetry and his daily life. Like Claudel's, his poetry is not only religious but Catholic in the narrow as well as in the broad sense of the word. Perhaps Maurois was led to include them because of their tough-minded yet tender and unchanging love for France, whose peasants, soil and intellect they so ably represent. It is also to be remembered that Maurois wrote these lectures while France lay under the heel of a conqueror, and he may have been influenced in his choice by the fact that Péguy gave his life in World War I and that Claudel spent his entire life in his country's service as a diplomat. Be that as it may, Maurois deals tenderly with both poets. Péguy's poetry is explained somewhat less than Claudel's, obviously because it is easier to understand. Claudel is given a fuller treatment. The famous Claudelian *verset*, with its relation to the exhalations of the breath is explained. His plays are discussed in their turn, and each one is related to events and ideas that affected the poet's life. There is some *explication de texte* in both essays, but the lecturer refrains almost entirely from critical evaluation or a comparison of the poets' work with that of other poets.

An additional lecture, given in France, has sometimes been published with the foregoing. It deals with Paul Valéry who would have required a more painstaking analysis than the first two if the lecturer had wished to make his audience understand a difficult subject. Evidently he felt that a single lecture could not accomplish such an end, and so he contented himself with an amiable discussion of Valéry's intellectual outlook. He sees him as a man who, like Descartes, had the courage to throw away all received ideas and make a fresh start. Valéry, he says, is aware that we cannot know the infinite. What we live on are conventions, tacitly agreed upon, and this fact makes civilized life possible. He describes Valéry's life and the dreary occupations that accompanied the intense activity of his mind. He tells with relish how Valéry pointed to texts from Hugo and Musset and called them obscure just to show, paradoxically, that his own work was not really difficult. This is a charming lecture which Maurois thought enough of to publish first as a separate book, but it fails utterly to examine Valéry's difficult writing. Its charm is, therefore, a kind of snare, for the apparent ease of Maurois' discussion masks the fact that he has entirely avoided the problem of understanding Valéry. The reader of the essay is informed about some of the Valéry's ideas, but he has yet to face the problem of comprehending his poetry. This is the biographical method at its worst in literary criticism, for of all the poets we read today Valéry is probably least understandable in terms of his biography.[49]

The discussion of André Gide is similarly incomplete. Gide is also introduced through the medium of his life story. There can be no quarrel about this, but the elucidation of that life in terms of his work is only superfically provided. Gide's Protestantism, puritanism, and childhood revolt are discussed intelligently, and his resulting need for self-realization is made plain. We follow him to North Africa where he managed to rid himself, so he alleged, of his guilt complex. We are told how he came to write *Nourritures terrestres* with its concluding phrase, "Families, I hate you." Gide's life and work are explained as products of a belated and continuing adolescence. For this reason, says Maurois, Gide was able as a grown man, possessed of a grown man's talent, to write as younger men write. And this, he says, explains the popularity of Gide with a whole generation of young people in France. All this, so far as it goes, is true and is well known to anyone possessed of the most superficial knowledge of Gide and his work; but it is difficult to forgive Maurois for failing to come to grips with Gide's novels. His failure to do so makes of his essay an unsatisfactory biography in the form of literary criticism.

The attempt to clarify the philosophy of Henri Bergson in a brief lecture was also doomed to accomplish something less than was intended; in his essay, however, Maurois wasted no time in tackling the problem. Eschewing for the occasion his penchant for biographical detail, he begins forthwith to explain in simple terms the essence of Bergson's philosophy. Bergson called the body a machine used by the soul. By this he meant that the soul is the creative center of life, and he adds that we may as well call this center God. Maurois explains how Bergson came to realize that without God, or a life principle, there is no way to explain the universe. Mechanistic explanations he rejected along with what he regarded as the tiresome atheism of the nineteenth century. He then found himself thrown back upon something other than reason, a something to which reason must yield. His conclusion was that the soul exists, that God exists, and that the *élan vital*, "or life force," must be reckoned with. Maurois did a fairly good job in this essay with a difficult task. But he is more at home with the novel and with novelists.

Maurois' lecture on Mauriac is one of his best. He relates him first of all, sensibly and intelligently, to his Jansenist background. He describes his early reaction against the pecuniary standards of the Bordeaux bourgeoisie from which he came. It was this reaction, he says, that accounts for Mauriac's hatred of the hypocritical society in which he lived and which he attacked in his novels. He discusses the relation between the damnation of the characters of Mauriac's novels and the novelist's own personal belief in the saving power of God's grace. He does not find room to analyze individual novels in detail, but his discussion of the ensemble of Mauriac's work is sufficiently provocative, so that after hearing it, a student is equipped to read Mauriac intelligently for himself. What he accomplished in this essay is, or should be, the purpose of all such essays.

Duhamel, Romains, and Martin du Gard are well handled also. In each essay the major share of the discussion is devoted to the long novels: *Salavin* and *La Chronique des Pasquier* in the case of Duhamel; *Les Hommes de bonne volonté* in the case of Romains; and *Les Thibault* for Roger Martin du Gard. In all these our critic finds fine writing to admire. Duhamel, he says, demonstrates through his characters that life has no easy solutions to offer. The relatively successful Laurent Pasquier has as many insoluble problems confronting him as does the weak and helpless Salavin. The meaning of the Thibault family's problems he sees as quest for certainty in a world in which nothing like certainty can exist. He draws attention in passing to Martin du Gard's statement that writing should not have to be talked about: "If I have to explain what I have written, I have not done my job properly." But it is for Jules Romains that Maurois reserves his highest praise. In *Les Hommes de bonne volonté* he finds some of the best writing of the twentieth century, and he adds that no one, not even Balzac, has known intimately so many phases of the life of his time. In all these essays detailed analyses of plots and characters are avoided in favor of guidelines for the understanding of the work of the author as a whole.

The discussion of Jacques de Lacretelle, the dilettante who finally turned to authorship, gives Maurois one of his rare occasions for speaking of the place of the Jew in modern society, and he makes the most of his opportunity. He contends that, for the most part, novelists who have written about Jews have not known what they were talking about. He regards Lacretelle's *Silberman* as a conspicuous exception. He says that in this novel, as in Proust and in Duhamel, the Jew is adequately and sympathetically treated. He also regards Lacretelle's other novels as worthy of praise, and his analysis of them leads him to the conclusion that he is one of the better novelists of the period between wars.

Saint-Exupéry had a special place in Maurois' heart. In a period when most novelists were tearing man down, Saint-Exupéry alone was engaged in building him up. He repeats from Saint-Exupéry the oft-quoted line to the effect that no animal lost in the Andes as was the flier Guillaumin would have had the courage and fortitude to work his way back to civilization as he did. This statement is cited as a sample of Saint-Exupéry's faith in man. In Maurois' view this faith was the most important thing in the flier's life. Next came devotion to duty, a quality to be defined quite without reference to any notion of morality or simple adherence to a code of ethics. Added poignancy is given to this essay by the fact that it was written just when the news had come that Saint-Exupéry's plane had been lost over the Mediterranean.

The defects of this series of lectures, turned into essays, have already been noted in part, that is, an unwillingness in some instances to come to grips with the defects of an author's work, and, as a corollary, a tendency to dwell overly long on biographical details, whether relevant or not. As we have seen, Maurois sought to ward off this sort of criticism by saying that he chose to discuss authors whom he knew well and liked. By so doing, he believes that he was enabled to achieve solidarity with his subject in a way that would otherwise have been impossible. Even so, the writers of Maurois' choice can hardly have been perfect. We know they were not, either personally or as writers, and we tend to feel that in literary criticism too much praise must be accounted a flaw. In contrast to Maurois' mild practice, Sainte-Beuve comes once again to mind, for the latter had the necessary stiffness of backbone to evaluate friend and foe alike. But Maurois was tender even with Sainte-Beuve in his biographical sketch of him. It is to be feared that Maurois' personal relationships with the men of whom he writes occasionally inhibited his pen. A more judicious course of action and one more in the interest of the writers in question would have required him to expose their flaws, for by so doing he would have made their virtues all the more plain. But Maurois, ever the man of peace and accommodation, finds it difficult to criticize his fellows harshly. The critical essays also contain not infrequent errors of fact both in the biographical and the analytical sections, thereby giving evidence of haste which, if forgivable on the lecture platform, should have been rectified before publication.

To later editions of the *Etudes littéraires* Maurois has added essays on André Malraux, Albert Camus, Jean-Paul Sartre, and Simone de Beauvoir. The Malraux essay is a little more cut and dried than the others. After a brief biography, which pays special attention to the writer's intelligence and to his many-sided achievements, Maurois calls him a man of action, meaning by this, apparently, that his novels are not the imaginings of a parlor strategist but the product of an experience which included the sweat and discomfort of the events that he chronicles. *Malraux was there.* This, Maurois thinks, gives his novels their special flavor and significance. Philosophically he believes that Malraux' whole life has been "a search for the absolute." He praises his superb technical competence in several fields and his way of dealing with an absurd world. He notes in passing that Malraux seldom writes of love except as a form of eroticism, and that when he writes about business matters, he is as competent as Balzac. This is praise but without any overtone of affection. From it one gathers that while Maurois admires Malraux' achievements and wants to give him his due as a moving and competent writer, neither the man nor his work are favorites of his.

The article on Camus is similarly ambivalent. As a non-existentialist, Maurois has some difficulty in appearing sympathetic toward existentialist philosophy, and so his treatment of Camus is a little forced. The Maurois method, however, comes to his rescue. He asks himself how Camus became what he was. He examines his humble background as a boy and young man in North Africa, and then he views the novels, plays, and essays as an outgrowth of ideas acquired while he was maturing. He observes that Camus was fascinated by the myth of Sisyphus and that from it drew not only the philosophical essay of that name, but also his novel *La Peste*. He notes that Camus disliked having his name coupled with that of Sartre with whom he had had a quarrel that led to a break between them. Maurois regards Camus as most unlike Sartre in that, though he sees the world as godless, he insists that, for his own good, man must continue to struggle onward. Sartre and Simone de Beauvoir are given similarly short analytical treatment.

III *Marcel Proust*

In many ways, chronologically and otherwise, Maurois' long work on Marcel Proust, aptly titled *A la recherche de Marcel Proust* (1949), is the culmination of his career as a literary critic. Most reviewers have treated the work as yet another biography, and one American translation has as its subtitle "A Biography." Yet little or nothing about this work relates it to the kind of work that Maurois has been calling "biography." Proust's work rather than his life dominates the book, and it is only by refusing to distinguish between Maurois' literary criticism and his biography that this study can be made to fit into the latter category. Jacques Suffel, Maurois' biographer, hints at this when he says perceptively: "This time the writer avoided the strict stance of biography." [50] Other critics, however, have failed to make this distinction.

Prior to the publication of this long and serious work on Proust, Maurois had shown his interest in him by other essays. Fairly buried in a scholarly volume of *English Studies*, "published by the members of the English Association" in Great Britain, is a little piece of research entitled "Proust et Ruskin," written early in his career (1932). He calls attention to the fact that Proust translated Ruskin and that in his great work he mentions him frequently and admiringly. Acting on this knowledge, scholars everywhere might have been expected to come forward to put Proust under a magnifying glass in order to learn the actual extent of Ruskin's influence. Few seem to have done so, and Maurois' short essay attempts to do the job. After investigation he was able to show convincingly that Proust was not only indebted to Ruskin for certain aspects of his style, which he demonstrates by comparisons, but that he took from Ruskin certain important attitudes toward life and art. Rejecting the notion that one must see nature or art without an intermediary, Proust accepted Ruskin's idea that our impressions are learned rather than innate, and he confesses that in his own case Ruskin determined for him the form that his impressions were to take. This is a stimulating and thoughtful article which suggests among other things how productive and useful a scholar Maurois could have been had he chosen a full-time academic career.

His second attempt to explain Proust was a lecture he gave to his American college audiences. This lecture is one of the best in his *Etudes littéraires*. Like the longer work to come, it spends little time on biography but tries to show the meaning of involuntary memory as the expression is used by Proust, and he shows how this differs from the voluntary memory that constitutes the greater part of most books of memoirs. He describes the vast plan of Proust's novel and makes fun, by implication, of those who mistake his way of writing for aimless and undirected rambling. He analyzes at some length Proust's concept of love as a kind of malady in which the beloved is merely a projection of qualities within the lover, and he points out that this implies that any degree of fulfilment of a desire causes an automatic diminution in the emotion of love. Albertine's cheek, for instance, when kissed, becomes far less desirable than the same cheek when the narrator merely hoped to kiss it. But, adds Maurois, this is not the only sort of love that exists. Proust's narrator, in describing his fondness of his grandmother, amply documents a quite different sort of emotion.

Without dwelling unduly upon Proust's hypochondria, our author describes the unhygienic habits that helped to bring him to an early death. We see his neurasthenia as an unhealthy extension of a sensibility that requires him not merely to look at a bouquet of roses but to study it intensely in order to extract the fullest measure of enjoyment from his sensations. This is an excellent short article, by far the best in the volume in which it was published; but it was only the beginning of a long interest in Marcel Proust.

By his second marriage to Mlle Simone de Caillavet, Maurois was led quite naturally to a deep and abiding interest in Proust and his work, and his long study went far beyond the relatively few hours necessary to the preparation of a short article. He had earlier amused himself by writing a pastiche of Proust's style which he

called *Le Côté de Chelsea,* even as Proust had amused himself in
his youth by imitating the style of others. Maurois' short piece on
Proust is seldom mentioned and is apparently little read or studied,
although it deserves to be read purely for its entertainment value.
The imitation is a double spoof. While imitating Proust's long sentences and involved view of things, Maurois was commenting in a
satirical though kindly fashion on English society. Like most persons
who attempt a stylistic imitation of another man's writing, Maurois
discovered that the task was more difficult than he had imagined.
In any event the writing of *Le Côté de Chelsea* was but one of a
number of points of contact with *A la Recherche du temps perdu*
that made him wish to study both the work and its author more at
length. An additional and perhaps deciding factor was his wife's
possession of a number of Proust's papers that had never before
been available to biographers or critics. With these in hand, he made
up his mind to do a full-length study of Proust and his work.

The biographical portion of the book is short. After a scant dozen
pages in which the story of Marcel's sickly and tortured physical
existence is sympathetically but quickly disposed of, we are launched
upon a study of the works. Thereafter such biographical details as
are supplied have their use mainly in explaining the great novel.
This is a new procedure for Maurois. Previously he had held to the
notion that to understand a man's work we should first know all
about him. For most critics this has been especially true of Marcel
Proust. Biographers and critics have said that without an intimate
knowledge of Proust's sheltered upbringing, his egotistical desire to
shine in the highest society, his manias and his illnesses, particularly
his asthma, only a superficial understanding of his writing is possible.
In this book Maurois has almost reversed the process. The study of
the works reveals to us a great deal about the author, but our attention is drawn to the latter by the former.

Another notable feature of this study is the fact that Maurois'
attitude toward his subject comes close at times to hero worship.
We are well acquainted with his dictum that in order to write a
successful book about a man, one should have a modicum of respect
and admiration for him; but this is the first time he has gone so far
in praise. Nor can his sympathy be attributed solely to the fact that
he was distantly related to him by marriage. The family connection
was perhaps not negligible, but of more obvious importance is his
expressed belief that the world has, in Proust's novel, one of the
great documents of our time, perhaps of all time, for an understand-

ing of the human condition. Significantly, too, Maurois keeps his own reactions to a minimum. From first to last the text of this book is accompanied by footnotes which have their source in papers and documents available to no previous student of Proust.

An unavowed but apparent aim of Maurois' lengthy critical work is to make Proust accessible to those who have hitherto neither liked nor understood him. The reading of his work is practically obligatory for literate Frenchmen, but there is little exaggeration in saying that he is mainly enjoyed and appreciated by a coterie of near worshippers, "the happy few." No intelligent student of literature has the audacity to pass him by, but he is often admired, as it were, *in absentia*.

In order to write of Proust intelligently, Maurois had to accept the prominence of homosexuality in his work. No one has taken a stand against Proust's right to deal with the subject, but even if this fact of life is now unblushingly admitted to discussion and even to prominence, it remains for many persons a clinical rather than a social phenomenon. Maurois meets the problem without flinching. Even the subject of Proust's personal inversion, and whether it be fact or mere inference, is dealt with in more detail and with more frankness than ever before. His conclusion is that Proust is guilty, but that his guilt is not very important. To reach this conclusion, Maurois resorts to the usual argument employed in such apologies. He holds that inversion is not inacceptable in itself, but that social attitudes make it so.

Another aspect of Proust that has caused him to be admired, but not widely popular, is the fact that his work deal almost entirely with upper-class social groups lacking universal interest and appeal. The psychology of the rich and idle, their secret vices, and the detailed description of *fin de siècle* Parisian society are regarded by many otherwise openminded readers as something like a museum piece, to be glanced at in passing, after which the visitor passes on to something of more vital interest. Maurois is evidently aware of this antipathy, frequently disguised as mere indifference, which is felt toward Proust by many readers, Frenchmen and foreigners alike. And so he devotes a long chapter to proving that Proust's subjects were more germane to everyday life than they appear to be after casual reading. This demonstration is lovingly and carefully prepared and will please Proustians. Whether it will convince the skeptical is another question. Maurois makes a case for Proust's human qualities and especially for his humor, a quality seldom mentioned in connection with him. Finally, for Maurois Proust is the supreme genius in his study of a segment of Parisian society, and through his study of that society a master of the art and science of psychology.

The concluding pages of the book are remarkable. Maurois demonstrates with sympathy and humor how Proust's insatiable desire for fame during his own lifetime drove him on. We see Proust's efforts to boost his literary reputation in ways that would be ludicrous if they were not pathetic. No absurdity was unthinkable. He wrote flattering reviews of his own books and sent them to periodicals. Some of his famous long letters were intended to persuade friends to propose him for the Goncourt prize or the prize of the French Academy. He suffered anguish at the thought that fame was not his, and he saw his most outlandish efforts in his own behalf as a race with death. We are asked to conclude that for all his absurdities, his hypochondria, and his manias Marcel Proust was a great man—*sui generis,* of course—but a great man. And few who read this biography will disagree with that conclusion.

Critical reaction in America to this work of erudition and criticism was not unanimously favorable. It ranged all the way from Henri Peyre's sorrowful "one had a right to expect more" [51] to the laudatory conclusions of Joseph Wood Crutch who said:

M. Maurois' book, certainly the best single volume on the subject, is very likely to be the one to which subsequent writers will return both for its body of information and for the general outlines of what will probably be the standard portrait.[52]

In 1960, by a careful excerpting of this detailed study, Maurois published a charming and enlightening book entitled *Le Monde de Marcel Proust.* The text is made up of forty or more pages which relate the story of Proust. It is accompanied by a variety of large and small illustrations that show Proust's surroundings and depict him and his friends and associates. Several media are used: photographs, reproduced paintings, pen and ink sketches, and caricatures. To see this text is to know Proust better. Like the similar Hugo volume, it is invaluable for the student.

IV *Critical Prefaces*

Maurois' reputation in literary circles has often led to his selection as a writer of prefaces to new editions of classic books and authors, and he has regarded each of these prefaces as an occasion for an appreciative critical essay. Evidently he did not dislike the role of promoter of such publications, nor does he consider his contributions negligible, for in his collected works he has included eight of the more important of his prefaces. In some cases he had already had something to say about the author in question, but was attracted by the opportunity to add to or to modify his opinion. He was also pleased in several instances to have the opportunity of writing about an author he had not previously commented on, such as Jean-Jacques Rousseau. His preface was to be published at the head of a new edition of the *Confessions*. Two questions, says Maurois, dominate all else when we deal with this famous autobiography: (1) Was Rousseau as sincere as he pretended to be?; (2) What actually was the place of women in his life? Finding an answer to the first question interested Maurois greatly, for implied in the answer is the whole question of truth in biography. Rousseau had spoken of spurious sincerity, but his own work is so complicated that it is difficult to sort out the truth from the falsehood. Maurois' conclusion is that Rousseau could only tell the truth as he saw it, with a strong implication that his version was totally different from that of anyone else and that, given his neurasthenia, his truth was far from any sort of objective truth.

The question of Rousseau's relations with women is also complicated. It is known that he suffered from a malady of the bladder which made him nervous about being long in company, but this did not prevent him from being a sensualist, particularly in writing, since in this fashion he could compensate in imagination for his physical disability. Maurois credits Rousseau with being the first in French literature to sound his special kind of sensual yet tender note, and he further ventures to say that without him the later writings of Chateaubriand and Stendhal would have been impossible. The self-analysis of intimate feelings, begun by Rousseau, he sees reflected and developed in both René and Julien Sorel. The essay touches also on Rousseau's religion, his interest in music, and the tragic last days when he was beset by enemies both real and imaginary. In short, this brief discussion recreates Rousseau, the man and his works, in such an evocative fashion that the reader wants to read the book for himself. To accomplish this is no small feat, even though it is the admitted purpose of a literary preface.

At about the same time that he was writing about Rousseau, Maurois took on the task of evaluating and presenting to the public the philosophical *contes* of Voltaire. Once again he was attempting something he had seldom attempted before, that is, the analysis of a rationalist. It is less easy with Voltaire than with a Romantic like Rousseau to imagine the effect of a man's life upon his work. Were Voltaire's joys and sorrows, his triumphs and failures also sublimated in his writings? Maurois thinks so. He believes that the relative optimism of *Zadig* corresponds to a period of relative quiet for Voltaire while he was living with Madame du Châtelet. In parallel fashion the period after her death was more difficult for Voltaire, and so he was moved to write the less cheerful *Micromégas* which, though it mocks the pretentions of mankind, is in its way a praise of man. It points out that even such microscopically minute creatures as we are have managed, despite our insignificance, to accomplish a number of scientific miracles. Finally, with *Candide*, Voltaire offers little in the way of ultimate joy or salvation for mankind, yet still refuses to give way to total pessimism, declaring that in the absence of philosophical certainties we may as well enjoy life as best we can. Voltaire is no exception to Maurois' rule that he writes only about persons who interest him and for whom he feels some sympathy, but his treatment of Voltaire is a shade less enthusiastic than his treatment of Rousseau or Shelley. It is to be noted in passing that Maurois in this essay allowed himself a quiet dig at the existentialists, who are otherwise little mentioned in his writings. He says that Voltaire discovered long before they did that the world is absurd, and concludes: "In *Candide* Voltaire has written all that can be thought upon the subject, and he did so wittily, which is better than being irritated thereby, and it leaves some courage for action." [53]

Maurois also wrote a preface for a Voltaire anthology entitled *Les Pages immortelles de Voltaire*.[54] In this essay he examines, somewhat more in detail, Voltaire's philosophy and theology, and he finds his ideas helpful in understanding the man, though wanting in particulars. Voltaire, he says, never seems to have noticed that, unlike himself, many people need some kind of spiritual nourishment and that if the exhortation to cultivate one's garden is sufficient for some men at some times, it is not sufficient for all men at all times. There are moments, says our author, when men need to be distracted from their gardens in order to rise up and resist fanatics of a sort Voltaire neither knew nor imagined. The essay is sparkling and shrewd both for what it says about Voltaire and for the way that his times are related to our own.

La Bruyère was another of the pessimistic rationalists on whom

Maurois agreed to comment. Obviously he was disappointed to recall that little or nothing of the philosopher's humdrum life comes through in his writings, but he says, gamely, let us see what can be deduced from his writing alone. He notes that La Bruyère was a cynic like Julien Sorel, but he warns us that the resemblance stops there. What appears to please Maurois most in the *Caractères* is the fact that men of today still closely resemble the portraits of those who lived so long ago. He is also pleased to remark that La Bruyère was one of the first in his time to sympathize with the masses of the people.

Maurois had admitted more debt to Balzac than to Flaubert, but he shares with his literate countrymen a deep and abiding admiration for *Madame Bovary*, which the French like to think of not merely as the greatest French novel, but as the greatest novel of modern times. Maurois notes the slowness with which the novel was written, but remarks that careful composition does not make a masterpiece in and of itself. He finds it curious that *Madame Bovary*, like *Don Quixote*, should be an anti-romantic novel. For Maurois the greatest single fact about Flaubert is his determined attack upon the concept of romantic love. This idea, says Maurois, after developing in the Middle Ages continued to increase in importance and prestige until during the Romantic period love was the greatest single fact of life. This prestige is what Flaubert set out to destroy. He was also proud of the fact that he had made a long novel out of a trifling incident. "What I want to do," he said, "is to write a book about nothing . . . a book which will hold up because of the inward strength of its style." And this he did. Maurois describes the famous morals trial that Flaubert had to undergo as the result of the publication of his novel. He depicts him as disgusted by the whole performance and particularly annoyed that the public should be romantic enough to imagine that it knew enough about art to condemn, or even to praise, the work of a literary artist. Maurois' conclusion is that *Madame Bovary* is the finest work of literature since Balzac.

This last qualifying phrase is an interesting one. Maurois has always admired Balzac enormously and, as already noted, he compares him to Shakespeare. The preface that he wrote for a new edition of *César Birotteau* was therefore a labor of love, and although it was written some years after his critical essay on Balzac, it antedates by some time his Balzac biography. In analyzing the action of the novel, Maurois points out, as every critic must, the disparity between Balzac the near-bankrupt, who failed in all his business ventures, and Balzac the novelist who knew how to depict coldly and accurately the errors of judgment which made other people fail. Maurois' highest praise for Balzac is that he refrained from judging his own characters. He makes them live, but he does not sit in judgment upon them, and in this self-restraint lies greatness. Great also was his failure to reward virtue and punish vice in the sentimental but unrealistic manner of Dickens. Maurois believes that *César Birotteau* is the greatest novel on business ever written, and he quotes Alain to the effect that it should be required reading in business schools. In every line of this preface Maurois' fondness for Balzac shows through. Balzac is held up as the model for novelists.

Later on, Maurois wrote a similar introduction for *Le Père Goriot* in which he dwells even more successfully on Balzac's method. For Maurois, *Goriot* marked the change from the writer of many novels to the composer of a carefully plotted series of social studies in novel form to be called the *Comédie humaine*. Maurois is at his best here, and his introduction can be recommended to young persons who are about to begin their reading of Balzac. It will interest Americans to know that the idea of having characters appear and reappear in successive novels was borrowed from James Fenimore Cooper, but the idea of using this device to create a well-knit, interrelated world was Balzac's own. It was his skill in creating a world of his own that makes him the novelist that he is. Others created unrelated slices of life. Balzac, by his interrelated characters, established his claim to greatness.

A request for a preface to a new edition of the *Mémoires d'outre-tombe* brought Maurois back again to Chateaubriand. In his biography he had relied heavily, if cautiously, on this work, and he was therefore intimately acquainted with it. Within the limits already described he admired it as a work of art. He begins his preface with this provocative statement:

Chateaubriand dominates the history of French literature in the nineteenth century like a snow-covered range which is so vast that one can travel over the entire country without ceasing to see its white peaks on the horizon.[55]

To justify this remark, he shows that Chateaubriand had a part in most of the historical happenings of his lifetime. Surprisingly he admires Chateaubriand's style, which even for some French critics is pompous as well as stately. For Maurois it has an irresistible charm.

He observes Chateaubriand's fondness for women and hints that even this is a charming trait. He thinks him sublime rather than ridiculous as he stands gravely listening to the reading of his memoirs in Madame Récamier's salon. He excuses the hypocrisy with which Chateaubriand sold the rights to his memoirs, only to protest when they were published. Above all, Maurois wished to convince his readers that the memoirs are frequently charming, and to do so he provides many judiciously chosen quotations. But the initial statement concerning Chateaubriand's dominance is a little extreme if we consider the number of equally great men to whom Maurois has called attention in his biographies. Maurois seldom repeats himself, but in this essay he borrows verbatim from his earlier biography.

Maurois' role as a teacher in American universities led him to venture away from the nineteenth century which, judging by his devotion to it, was his favorite historical period. He ventured less often into the eighteenth century, although his writing on La Bruyère, Rousseau, and Voltaire showed that he was equally at home in other periods. Still his preface to an edition of the memoirs of the Cardinal de Retz seems almost like an accidental journey into the seventeenth century. He begins with an excellent thumbnail sketch of his subject, since he does not assume, as he does with Flaubert and Voltaire, that his reader is already familiar with the main outlines of his subject's biography. He then discusses the Cardinal's political theories, comparing him favorably with Machiavelli and Stendhal. He tells his readers that they will derive pleasure from reading the prelate's memoirs, and his preface is intended to prepare them to do so. Maurois has done his homework well.

V *Obiter Dicta*

In 1946 Maurois published in the United States a book with the ambiguous title *Five Faces of Love*. In a later French edition, and with the addition of two chapters, it became *Sept Visages de l'amour*. At first glance the work is hard to classify. As he begins the book, the reader is likely to believe that Maurois embarked on a history of the concept of love, since the introductory chapter contains such a résumé. Beginning with the ancients, Maurois demonstrates that their idea of passion, their concept of fidelity, and their matrimonial customs gradually evolved into the altogether different romantic love exemplified by Tristan and the knights of the Middle Ages. According to him, both feudalism and Christianity had a hand in this transformation. Coming down to the seventeenth century, he shows how even rough soldiers, when they had turned courtier, became interested in the love casuistry of such novels as *Clélie* and *Astrée,* although in real life passion and its manifestations were considerably cruder than they were depicted in literature. After concluding these preliminary remarks, he sums up the life of Madame de Lafayette, a woman whom he describes as separated from her husband, although the latter loved her dearly. He declares that she wrote the *Princesse de Clèves* as a mirror of the society in which she lived, and he shows how the love affair that it describes belongs unmistakably to the period. He analyzes the novel in a classroom manner, quotes illustrative passages from it, and comments on the style. The result is an unrewarding if unpretentious essay. Everything that is said in the context has been said before, and better, either by Maurois himself or by others.

The second chapter, which discusses *La Nouvelle Héloise* is a great deal more penetrating. Maurois remarks that the eighteenth century was a cynical period in which the passions were seldom hidden. Therefore, because of their contrast with the exaggerated realism of society, Rousseau's protestations in favor of absolute purity were widely appreciated. His protagonists, Saint-Preux and Julie, he tells us, were models for both Napoleon and Stendhal. Rousseau brought natural goodness to the fore, and though moral practices were not actually changed thereby, he held up to society at least a higher standard than it pretended to follow.

The chapter which follows deals with the heroines of Stendhal, whose life was so accurately reflected in his works. Maurois sees Stendhal as trying to recreate in his novels the mistresses of real life. And what he thought they were like and what they really were presents a striking contrast. Stendhal professed to like women to tremble and sigh. In their company he liked to vaporize and theorize after the manner of Werther. This is why in *Le Rouge et le noir* he created the tender Madame de Rénal and contrasted her with the wilful and passionate Mathilde, each of them representing a type of woman that he admired. In his analysis of the novel, Maurois says that Stendhal was sympathetic toward the emotion of jealousy and that he felt a tremendous scorn for everything in life that was unrelated to love. In his own way he was as romantic about love as Rousseau, and though he wrote of it in the style of the *Code Napoléon,* he is still read and admired while the sentimental Rousseau is not. This is an excellent essay.

The chapter on *Madame Bovary* was written three years after the introductory preface alluded to above, but it is quite different from it. In this instance Maurois devoted much time to Flaubert's life and to his liaison with Louise Colet. He sees Flaubert as having to struggle against a romantic tendency in himself, and he suggests that *La Tentation de Saint-Antoine* was the story of that struggle. In analyzing *Madame Bovary* Maurois reveals that he was writing primarily for an American audience by remarking that Madame Bovary is with us everywhere today, in America as elsewhere. He comments with wry humor that she would have made a good wife for the pharmacist Homais.

The last chapter, entitled "Les Héroines de Marcel Proust," foreshadows his later critical study. Proust, he tells us—and he was later to repeat this in a preface to the novelist's letters—perceives love as pain and as an anguish to be cured rather than endured or enjoyed. A case in point is Swann who wasted himself on a woman of a type he did not really like. His is an extreme case, but Maurois feels, as he would be bound to feel after writing chapters on four other kinds of love, that Proust's concept of love is only a partial one. The novelist was further handicapped by choosing to describe a variety of love that was experienced by an idle and wealthy society, and so we cannot accept his analysis as complete. The readers of Maurois' book-length study of Proust are bound to find this discussion repetitious. He must have realized this fact because he refrained from including these remarks in his complete works.

As a conclusion to his volume, Maurois summarizes as follows the kinds of love depicted by his five authors:

In sum Madame de Lafayette had studied love like a metaphysician, Rousseau like a moralist, Stendhal like a man in love, Flaubert like an unbeliever and an iconoclast. Proust studied it both as a poet and a medical practitioner.[56]

A later edition adds two other kinds of love to this picture: the eighteenth-century version of illicit passion, described in *Les Liaisons dangereuses* by Choderlos de Laclos, and the kind of love that Balzac ascribes to his heroines.

The reviews that greeted these literary essays went from mild condemnation to mild praise. Few reviewers took the trouble to assign them to their proper category as literary criticism of the popular sort; instead, they dismissed them as a collection of random essays. The title, of course, was misleading. Still Maurois received a few left-handed compliments. August Derleth, for instance, writing in *Book Week,* referred to an "occasional profundity hidden beneath Maurois' light manner," and goes on to say that he rather likes the book on the whole.[57]

Viewed from the perspective of literary criticism and compared with Maurois' other critical works, this book on the novels of passion is of minor interest. Viewed as classroom lectures in print, it is neither the best nor the worst of its sort. It is easy reading, and if it has whetted any appetites for reading the books that are discussed, it has served its purpose.

Maurois found an excellent outlet for the critical function in the opinions that he wrote as a member of the Book-of-the-Month Club jury. He collected these short reviews in a book called *Etudes améri-caines.* As required by the Club, these pieces had to be of a more-or-less uniform length and written to a set formula. Their purpose was to persuade the membership to purchase the current selection, and their general tenor was expected to be laudatory. These rules observed, each reviewer had free rein to write as he liked. Unkind critics call such essays a "blurb," which is what they usually are. In Maurois' case they are always more than that. In every instance he made a serious effort to explain an author's purpose and to reveal his outstanding qualities. He was called upon to write about such disparate items as *The Collected Short Stories of Dorothy Parker* and John Dos Passos' *The State of the Nation.* He always did the job well, though it must have been no easy task for a Frenchman, even one so well acquainted with the United States as Maurois, to understand the nuances of everything he read. Still, in each case, he wrote in an interesting and original manner, and his usefulness to the Club by his distinguished presence on the jury was equalled by his skill in presenting the new American books. He had the happy faculty of making it appear that each book that he read was a treat to him, and it was this quality of personal enjoyment and enthusiasm which made him so useful in America as a popularizer of French literature and French ideas, and so useful in France as an interpreter of America.

In his own country the occasions for self-expression furnished by membership in the French Academy were not lost on Maurois. His speech of acceptance was an opportunity to rehabilitate the character of the crusty pedagogue and magazine editor René Doumic to whom Maurois owed much for his kindness and encouragement. One of his fellow academicians remarked that it was truly a stroke of genius to have found it possible to say something nice about the opinionated old gentleman.

A few years later, the admission of his friend Jean Cocteau to the Academy gave Maurois a chance to pay tribute to him as well as an opportunity to analyze and praise the works of the Tharaud Brothers, since it was the seat of Jérôme Tharaud that Cocteau was assuming. Similarly, as representative and spokesman for the Academy, Maurois spoke at a celebration of the centenary of the death of Lammenais. As usual, he prepared himself by becoming familiar with the details of his subject's life and works. Avoiding mere vapid and generalized praise, he gave a well-researched discussion of the priest's trials and tribulations and of his successes and influence.

From the foregoing it appears that the field of literary criticism came to occupy a prominent place in Maurois' work. He himself realized this, and after taking the first steps toward self-analysis in his lectures on the art and practice of biography, he was ready thereafter to talk about his own work. Thus in the prefaces which he wrote for each volume of his collected works we find some of his most penetrating analyses of his books. It is, for instance, in these prefaces that he provides many of his best critical opinions, as we have seen in connection with his novels and biographies.

It is these observations which lie buried, as it were, in the volumes of the collected works (where they are unlikely to be seen by any but the most fervent admirers of Maurois) that he fully reveals his stature as a critic as well as in some of his more widely read literary criticisms. Perhaps the key to his evaluations, as to most of what he wrote is this remark, which a careful perusal of his works proves to be literally true: "I am never satisfied to do a hasty or improvised job when asked to write or to speak."

CHAPTER 6

Side Excursions

OF all the writers who might be chosen for study, Maurois would be the least likely to be offended by the inclusion of a chapter on "Miscellaneous Writing." "I like so many things," he said, as if with a smile, and it is this almost universal curiosity of his which in an age of specialists and specialization makes his thoughts provocative and vital. To be interested in many things is to renounce a certain sort of erudition. Maurois did not make of himself a scholar like André Malraux, nor was he even a specialist on French society in his century as was Balzac. This he knew. He admitted that he had so enjoyed life in its many aspects, so enjoyed traveling, the lecture platform, the classroom and the kudos of the famous writer that he never had time to become either learned or deeply philosophical. Nor did he come to feel that certain kinds of literary endeavor were beneath his dignity. In his old age he was not above contributing prefaces to other writers' books if the subject interested him. For this willingness to lend his talent to many endeavors he was inevitably called a "dilettante." Certainly he sacrificed a greater reputation and a more refined skill to the demands of a busy and happy existence. He admitted as much. But he enjoyed sharing his interests with his readers in a variety of books that all but defy classification.

I *Alain Again*

The most serious of the miscellaneous works is his fairly long treatise on Emile Chartier, the teacher to whom he gave a lifetime of devotion. He had included a hasty sketch of him among his university lectures. He came back to him again in two essays, *Alain et le romanesque* and *Alain liseur,* but neither these brief tributes nor the innumerable references to Alain throughout his works appear to have satisfied him. He felt an urge to give Alain's philosophy separate and careful treatment, and he did so in an essay of some sixty-five pages. In it we are given to understand that Alain was primarily interested in modern society and its organization. Like many bachelors he held staunch convictions regarding the manner in which other people courted, married, begot children, raised children, quarreled, and were sometimes divorced. If he had a touch of anarchy in his socialistic view of the modern state, he was nevertheless a firm believer in the sanctity of the family. His method of communicating these ideas to his students was the Socratic dialogue which he kept firmly under control. He allowed no discussion. The master teaches and the students learn, he used to say. Maurois soaked all this up. It is little to be wondered at, therefore, that all his own works, whatever their classification, have to do with the problems of society. Christianity is a part of that society, and it is not without significance that when Jacques Suffel commented on Alain's influence in his author-critic dialogue, Maurois' rejoinder was to the effect that among Alain's gifts to him was an appreciation of Christianity.

Maurois' often expressed belief that individuals rather than masses, committees, or legislative bodies make history was exemplified in his own life by his relation to Alain. It was the high-school philosophy teacher who made the difference in his own case, who influenced his thinking and his behavior and through these molded his life to a liberal pattern it would otherwise not have had. Yet this influence was exercised by a not very well rounded philosophy. As Maurois knows, Alain's attitude toward authority was contradictory. He never reached any viable relationship with the society in which he lived. Until his death his individualism was so extravagant that he preferred to grant the government no powers even in behalf of the common weal. He was a kind of Platonist with Lockian tendencies and professed a completely unacademic kind of skepticism. These traits undoubtedly had a good effect on Maurois who, since he was born into a factory-owning family, might never have seen the workers' point of view if had not been for Alain. Still, as a practical mill executive meeting a payroll, Maurois learned to separate fact from theory and to see the economic structure from a vantage point denied to his teacher.

Regrettably this piece on Alain is far from one of Maurois' best, and if it is not good Maurois, one suspects that it is not good Alain either. Alain was a teacher, which is but another way of saying that his influence was best seen in the classroom. Despite Maurois' statements to the contrary, Alain was not a gifted writer, nor has he been widely read, and those who were not his students are incapable of imagining what his words must have sounded like as he faced a class and uttered them with all the force of a striking personality. If Maurois is to be believed, no one in Alain's classes ever forgot him or the ideas that he taught; yet an analysis of his philosophy, as it appears in his own books or in the frequent samples that Maurois has provided in quotations and epigraphs, fails to move the reader as they moved Maurois. The truth is that the pupil surpassed his master in every way. His sayings were pithier and more pregnant with meaning. One asks oneself why this should be so. Alain may have been every bit as good a teacher as Maurois says he was. He must have been magnetic in personality, dry in humor, contemptuous of fools, incisive in his questioning, and deft in repartee. But we have to take Maurois' word for this. The teaching process is difficult to record in the printed word for posterity. The tape recorder, invented since Alain's death, can help to convey the personality, charm, irascibility, and downright genius of a good teacher. A mere exposition of his words leaves out the peculiarities, great and small of his delivery, and these are the factors that convey his message. Yet Maurois has recreated for us the personalities of a score of persons, many of them long since dead, and we wonder why he could not repeat the miracle. Now Alain is gone and it must be accounted one of Maurois' failures that he did not succeed in kindling in his readers his own enthusiasm for him. Yet he has been indefatigable in his attempts to do so. Chapters of his books are frequently headed by epigraphs taken from Alain. Quotations from Alain abound at every turn. Nor did time dim the influence of his teacher's personality on Maurois. The man himself we see but dimly. His achievement was to make his students conscious of society and it problems.

II *The Good Society*

Maurois' first didactic approach to the problems of men and women in a modern society and the complex interplay of social relations is to be found in a treatise in the form of aphorisms entitled *La Conversation* (1927). As one reads these sayings, the maxims of La Rochefoucauld come instantly to mind, and one fears that Maurois, like previous imitators, will suffer by contrast. In point of fact, he does not. His aphorisms are well done. But why aphorisms in this day and age? There are several probable reasons for his trying his hand, not the least of which is the fact that a writer of proverbs must refine and sharpen his thinking as he refines and sharpens his prose. Such is the nature of the *genre* that the subtlest of thinking is unacceptable if it is not brilliantly presented, and, as a corollary, that a half truth may achieve immortality if the mold is striking. This sort of stylistic problem intrigued Maurois. He wanted to see if he could avoid banality while talking about what everyone else was talking about, and yet please and instruct at the same time. Paradox is a useful tool in such writing. So is a certain amount of cynicism. The result, as with the seventeenth-century master, is a cleverness of expression which sometimes hides the shallowness of the observation. Or if, as some philosophers allege, a maxim is seldom more than a half truth at best, then some of these maxims, like some of those of La Rochefoucauld, are less than half true. Still Maurois' maxims were read and admired when they appeared, though they have acquired little permanent reputation. Perhaps there is no room in a national literature for more than one writer of witty sayings.

Sentiments et coutumes (1934) continues Maurois' preoccupation with men, women and marriage. In an introductory chapter, which makes good use of literary allusions to marriage from Rabelais to Byron ("One can't live with women and one can't live without them."), he establishes the importance of marriage to modern as well as to former societies and discusses the problems that it brings in its wake. In a second chapter, entitled "Parents et enfants," he continues his urbane if not very profound discussion. He quotes Paul Valéry to the effect that families have a tendency to flee from each other, yet enjoy their daily communion around the dinner table. He refers his readers to famous families in French literature as for example Duhamel's Pasquiers. He calls attention to the terrible conduct of the two daughters, in Balzac's *Père Goriot*, which he contrasts with the happy family described in *Béatrix*.

The last two chapters of the treatise discuss friendship and happiness. Maurois' recipe for both is to cultivate the virtues of common sense and to avoid thinking too much about the past. This is an optimistic book, which had its origin in four public lectures. My purpose, says Maurois, was to "set forth in the simplest and most concrete terms some of the essential problems of living together in a household, in a family and in a modern state." [58] The probing is skillful and pleasant, but little more than that.

Un Art de vivre (1939) was a more pretentious effort along the same lines. The introduction describes the dilemma of human intelligence. Despite its importance, pure intellect is quite incapable of helping us to think logically about our passions. In analogical fashion human society cannot be expected to use the science of psychology to improve itself. Social circumstances are never altogether the same on any two occasions, and therefore the rigorous application of the scientific method cannot be effectively practiced in dealing with society. All that science can do for us is to stay ahead like a low-flying airplane spotting for artillery.

The second chapter, "Art d'aimer," offers little that is new. We have been over this ground before, whether in the writing of Maurois or elsewhere. Yet despite the triteness of the subject, the chapter is written engagingly and pleasantly, as most reviews agreed.

The "Art de travailler" continues the discussion, and here the former head of Elbeuf woolen mills appears to be speaking. He discusses the need for discipline on the job, for good working conditions, and for good relations between worker and employer.

The "Art de commander" adds nothing to what has already been said in the *Dialogues sur le commandement.*

The concluding chapter talks about the art of growing old. Maurois' advice to the reader is to continue to live well, to keep active in old age, and to maintain one's affections intact. He also cites the remarkable achievements of some very old men.

It is difficult not to be impatient with this book, impatient, in fact, with the whole series of books in which Maurois talks about life and advises his readers how to live it. For although he seldom pontificates and is almost never guilty of looking down on his reader, the writing of sententious essays would seem to be a strange way for a novelist and biographer to express himself. Readers have a right to expect the best of Maurois, free from personal pleading, in his novels and biographies. All that can be said in extenuation of these discursive productions is that our author has a delightful way of expressing himself. He reminds one at times of Fontenelle's discourses on astronomy which were addressed to a pretty young woman.

Very similar to the foregoing books is *Lettres à l'inconnue* (1953) which Maurois wrote to fulfill a journalistic commitment. Though largely a substantive repetition of his previous views on courtship, marriage, and a happy *modus vivendi* with the opposite sex, this book had several favorable reviews. The framework is provided by a weekly letter to an unknown young woman in which these questions are discussed amiably and wittily, but nothing more.

On two occasions Maurois found a far better vehicle than the casual essay for his ideas on sex and marriage: the drama. The skill that he displayed in these efforts makes one regret that he never made a serious attempt to conquer the theatre. In 1937 he made a translation with Virginia Vernon of Laurence Housman's *Victoria Regina* which had been successfully acted in Paris. For many years this was the closest he came to the theatre. Then in 1951, at the request of the French Broadcasting System, he wrote a scenario called *Cours de bonheur conjugal* in twelve scenes. The idea was suggested by his observation in the United States of college courses in "Domestic Relations" and "Marriage and the Family." Such courses struck Maurois as comical, and his radio play is an amusing spoof of such doings. The listener is asked to imagine himself observing a professor and his class. The subject is marriage. The professor introduces the topic for the day and then presents a playlet with living actors who act out a crisis in the married life of a couple named Marise and Philippe. When the scene is over the professor asks the students to comment. He then presents a second scene in which the marital blunders of the principals are rectified. The idea is amusing and ingenious, and at least one of the dialogues became the basis for the action of *Les Roses de Septembre,* published five years later.

In 1955 appeared *Aux innocents les mains pleines,* subtitled *proverbe en un acte.* In this cynical little playlet a mistress hoodwinks a wife and at the same time returns her husband to her affections. The plot and characters are amusing and clever, and once again the critics were led to wish that Maurois had devoted more time to drama.

III *Toward a Philosophy of Life*

With Maurois' demonstrated penchant for sharing his ideas with his public in lectures, essays, and articles, it is not to be wondered at that he published several books explaining his philosophy and his view on the world situation. The first volume in point of time was *Mes songes que voici* (1933) which consists of a series of meditations on randomly chosen subjects. He begins by examining the Mohammedan belief in fate, comparing it with the attitude of a banker who believes that the poor ought to be allowed to starve. Both the Mohammedan and the banker are fatalists, and fatalism, says Maurois, is no help in solving modern problems. Political and economic dilemmas are resolved only by those who have faith in their power to act and thereby to change conditions. In discussing the problems of Soviet Russia he says—and it must be remembered that this opinion was written more than thirty years ago—that as goods and services increase, the myth of anti-capitalism will subside and the zeal of the pioneer Communists will flag. As for himself, though no Utopian, Communist or otherwise, he believes that society needs constant change. Changes are even inevitable. They will come, and we can either choose to admit them gradually and control their direction or we can resist them and end up with revolution. For this reason the intelligent conservative, like Disraeli, aids and abets change. We need not fear change, says Maurois, and he quotes Huxley to the effect that, unlike Pascal, not all of us are afraid of the eternal silences of space. Nor do all of us fear immeasurably the possible loss of individual liberty as bureaucracy increases in size. Maurois looks to the future without fear and without borrowing trouble. He predicts a world with less work and more leisure. Twice in the course of these essays he imagines himself somewhere in space and able to contemplate the earth from a distance. Our planet is not without its beauty, he says, and his conclusion, if there is one, is that human life on earth may aspire to happiness. This is not profound philosophy, but then neither was it intended to be, as our author would probably have been the first to avow. He had many of these essays published separately in periodicals before they were collected into a volume.

An interesting addition to the foregoing exposition of Maurois' philosophical outlook is provided in the preface to the tenth volume of the *Oeuvres complètes*. In a brief essay he attempts a hard-hitting summary of the modern dilemma and its possible solutions. He observes, as many another has done, the contrast between the collective confidence of 1900 and the agony of Europe in 1950, faced with the possibility of self-destruction, possessor of vast knowledge and enormous material resources, the inventor of small gadgets and vast engines, but uncertain of its future and lacking entirely its former optimism. He then outlines a credo which gives the essence of his attitude toward life:

1. The real world exists.
2. Man has a mind.
3. I am not a pure materialist, since I cannot conceive how thought can be begotten of matter.
4. I find it difficult to hold the belief that man was made in God's image, and therefore I find myself a skeptic in religion.
5. To the skeptic the universe is neither friendly nor hostile.

6. God is that part of man that surpasses himself, but he is not a transcendent God.

7. There is no inevitability of a final catastrophe.

8. I believe in the rights of man and the separation of powers in government.

9. I reaffirm my belief in the old-fashioned virtues and in their value for human relations.

10. I believe in the value of art.

11. I see no inevitability of final punishment.

12. I advise each man to live as if he were immortal.

The virtue of this advice is its livability and its common sense, and it appealed to many of Maurois' middle-class readers.

As he grew older, Maurois' reputation for liberal opinions led him to the forefront of many a movement with which he had little or no desire to be connected. He was expected to make speeches for the furtherance of a diversity of causes. He was asked to edit all kinds of books or, at the very least, to write a foreword for a new book or for a new edition of a classic. Publishers and editors were well aware that the phrase "preface by André Maurois of the Académie française" was a stimulus to sales and that it assured at the very least an audience among the faithful. Sometimes, as we have seen, he was happy to indulge his weakness for praising his favorite books, and he mentioned that he had to guard against the constant temptation to take on more good causes and more literary chores than he could decently accomplish. He had to remember also that every extra job, whether presiding over a committee or writing a few paragraphs, deprived him of time which he ought to have devoted to creative work. Still there were invitations that he could not resist. Such a one was the invitation to say a word in behalf of UNESCO's work in establishing libraries. This piece he entitled *Public Libraries and Their Mission,* and it is just the sort of article that was expected of him. He makes an intelligent appraisal of the meaning to modern society of publicly accessible repositories of books and discusses their essentialness to the developing countries.

IV *Better than Ten Thousand Words*

Maurois is not unaware of the truth of the old Chinese proverb concerning the relative value of words and pictures, and so throughout the years the publication of copiously illustrated books has claimed a share of his time and attention. Undoubtedly his son

Gerald's skill as a photographer helped to turn him in this direction, but even before this influence could be brought to bear, he had been an enthusiastic lover of pictures. The books he has published to further this interest are many, ranging from guide books to histories and biographies, and they encompass most of his spectrum of interests. The first guide was called *Malte* (1935), a pictorial presentation for visitors to the island. The accompanying text gives the highlights of Maltese history and culture, and summarizes the problems encountered by Greek and Turk as they try to live together as a community. It deals also with the multiple facets of the island's daily life, and the accompanying pictures are as varied as they are beautiful.

In time he decided to repeat this type of venture, and five more guide books with accompanying text were successively published under his name. *Londres* (1936) followed quickly in the wake of Malta, but it was some twenty years later when *Paris* (1951), *Rio de Janeiro* (1954), *Périgord* (1955), and *Hollande* (1955) appeared. Each is a masterpiece of the photographer's art, and each contains a text that is lucid, urbane, and intelligent. *Versailles aux lumières* (1954) was a similar project. The palace had attracted Maurois' interest as a historian, and he wrote a pageant for performance there. A year later he published *Louis XIV à Versailles*, a delightful account of seventeenth-century life at court.

The presentation of masterpieces of art by means of illustrated books was a natural outcome of this sort of interest on Maurois' part. Already in 1939 he had written the text for an exhibition of English watercolors, entitled *Chefs d'oeuvres des aquarellistes anglais. Turner et ses contemporains.* Here for the first but not the last time Maurois essayed the role of art critic, discussing with warmth and skill the techniques employed in the watercolors which were reproduced in the book. He was to return to art several more times. As already noted, he had written, in 1948, a short children's biography of J. L. David, the sculptor. In 1952, as a result of his intimate association with the painter Fernand Léger while they were both teaching at Mills College, California, he prepared a text for a book of reproductions of Léger's paintings. Friendliness and geniality rather than serious art criticism is the tone of this little essay. In 1964 he composed the text for a portfolio of paintings by the Prince de Joinville, the son of King Louis Philippe of France. The prince, a young liberal, had been interested in the outcome of the American Civil War, and he spent more than two years with the Union armies observing and sketching. His watercolors are a useful document for the understanding of the war. Maurois' knowledgeable discussion of the situation in America during the war and of the Prince's political and military observations make interesting reading.

In 1931 Maurois agreed to present the Paris Colonial Exposition to the public in an illustrated volume. To illustrate the book, he used original lithographs by the artist Lagorce. Perusing this book nowadays, visitors to the exposition will remember nostalgically the pleasant and soon-to-vanish climate of Franco-African colonialism. In his text Maurois successfully recaptures the atmosphere of the exposition, and the illustrations recreate its scenes. Marshal Lyautey, who was the director-general of the exposition, kindly consented to write an introduction to the volume.

The considerable success and the undoubted popular appeal of his illustrated volumes led to Maurois' continued interest in such projects. In a class by itself is a curious volume of the year 1964 called *Femmes de Paris* in which every type of woman who lives in the city is pictured. The kaleidoscopic effect is dazzling. Maurois' text as usual is sparkling.

Possibly the most important use to which Maurois has put the photograph is in two of his latest histories. In 1955 he published *Histoire du peuple allemand* with illustrative material equal in bulk to the text itself. The result, as noted earlier, is an extremely brief history magnificently presented. The *Histoire d'Angleterre* was also issued in a special illustrated edition. But the most important illustrated volumes in Maurois' repertory of serious works are to be found in *Les Deux géants*, his contribution to the joint publication of a history of contemporary America and contemporary Russia by Louis Aragon and himself. The excellence of the text by Maurois has already been commented on. The illustrations deserve equal praise. An American unfamiliar with the French language would enjoy this searching camera exploration of his country, while, for the French reader, the pictures provide an unforgettable panorama.

V *Translations*

In the course of his career, Maurois essayed the task of translation several times, but he never set up any systematic program of translation or gave any indication that he intended to pursue it except occasionally and as the spirit moved him. His translation of *The Woman Changed into a Fox* and his translation of *Victoria Regina* seem to have been the product of impulse, and in both cases he sought bilingual collaborators. There remains one translation which he did by himself and which must have consumed a great deal of time and energy. This is his excellent rendering into French of *Sonnets from the Portuguese* (1946) by Elizabeth Barrett Browning. In his version Maurois succeeds in retaining, as a good translator should, the mood, the thought, and the spirit of the original. The fact that he should have tried to do so and that he should have succeeded are some cause for wonder, for he himself had never sought reputation as a poet. With the exception of a few verses written during World War I and which come from the supposed pen of the interpreter Aurelle, he has published no poetry. The Brownings, however, interested him, and he evidently wished to add to his biographical sketch of Elizabeth and her husband some study of the wife's poetry. For this reason he made it available in translation to the reading public of France.

From the foregoing remarks it is obvious that the range of Maurois' interests is as broad as he has said it is. From the point of view of severe critics he made a mistake in trying to encompass so much. If he had not dissipated his talents with casual essays, translation, picture books, and diaries, the suggestion is, he might have turned out more novels. Or he might have had more leisure to reflect, and the quality of his more important works might have benefited thereby. Maurois had thought about this himself. He saw in retrospect that traveling took an inordinate amount of his time, but he consoled himself with the thought that he never aspired to write a novel a year anyway, as some of his contemporaries have done. The truth is that though Maurois was not a man to let his career take its own direction, he was a man who intended to enjoy life, so that he never regarded a detour to examine something that caught his fancy along life's path as an intrusion upon more serious purposes. He welcomed side excursions for their own sake, and the books that have had their origin in detours from the narrow path of biography or fiction are frequently delightful, always entertaining. Maurois has no reason to deny them his approval.

CHAPTER 7

The Best of Two Worlds

CONSIDERING the proximity of France to her English-speaking neighbor across the Channel, the number of French schoolboys who major in English in the lycées is small. Before World War I it was smaller still. Fewer yet were the English majors whose choice of a vocation led them into teaching or any other field which kept alive their interest in British culture or in the English language after school days were over. André Maurois was to prove a brilliant and unexpected exception. It is tempting to try to account for his interest in English in pseudo-scientific fashion by deducing that a boy raised in a bilingual home might be expected to be more interested in language study than one from a monolingual background. Such explanations are highly suspect, however, for many a boy, in France and elsewhere, is not only totally uninterested in language study, but even refuses to speak or to understand the second language of his parents. For reasons of status he will speak only the national language. Thus the fact that the Herzog family spoke an Alsatian variety of German in addition to French may have been quite without influence on Emile. But this fact we know, that he decided, perhaps because he liked his teacher, to learn English, and by the time his school days were over, he could handle himself adequately if imperfectly in the language, and could understand it reasonably well. We have already seen how this skill, duly noted by the French army, led to his assignment to the post of interpreter. This experience, coming as it did a few years after he had left school for the mill, reawakened in the young man the interest in the British which had been kindled earlier by his studies. It did more than that. It aroused in him an unshakable curiosity about the Anglo-Saxon world, a curiosity which in time was to extend to America and to provide him with a basis for the study of the non-French world.

This curiosity was to last Maurois all his life. It was to make of him a cosmopolitan in the truest sense of the word. In his adult years, though he never could nor ever would renounce his allegiance to France, he found himself completely at home away from his own country. He liked to observe foreign ways and he was not constrained to apply narrow and purely French yardsticks to the measurement of alien cultures. Such detachment neither a Gide, nor a Romains, nor a Duhamel could achieve. Nor was Maurois' cosmopolitanism like the internationalism of Romain Rolland. The latter so ardently desired peace and comity between France and Germany that he was prepared to work with the men of many nations in the interest of peace. But he always remained a Frenchman, speaking French, and knowing actually very little about the Germany with which he wished to reconcile his own country. Maurois during his travels is far less concerned with political and international issues, though he is not unmindful of them. He enjoys new surroundings and his interpretation of Anglo-Saxon culture in France is based on knowledge and experience. He also enjoys the role of interpreter of France abroad, and for this and critic Jean Schlumberger has called him admiringly "the best ambassador of French letters to the Anglo-Saxon countries." [59]

I *England: A Second Country*

Maurois' wartime friendship with British officers was to be followed by peacetime contacts, some of which began in a curious way. It was his somewhat strange notion that his young fiancée would be better prepared for life if she completed her education in England. Naturally, after he had placed her in a school there, he was bound to pay her frequent visits, and so for a time he found himself practically commuting to England. In the process he acquired a familiarity with the country born of frequent contact, and this familiarity laid a solid basis for his study of the English character. As time went on, these contacts with persons and places in England were augmented by studies undertaken in English libraries in order to write his biography of Shelley, a project which required the reading of hundreds of books in English. Maurois thus steeped himself in the lore of nineteenth-century Britain. He became acquainted in detail with the life of the great universities, Oxford and Cambridge, from the former of which Shelley had been expelled. The bonds between Maurois and Britain were further tightened by the formation of the close friendships with young Englishmen and the reading of the biographies of Lytton Strachey, whom for a time he took for a model in his work. It was with this background that Maurois accomplished in real life what his fictional counterpart, Bernard Quesnay, was to do in the novel of the same name. He urged the ultraconservative, black-coated patriarchs who ran the family business to expand their dealings to include the English market, thus breaking for the first time with the hoary tradition of the family that "foreigners" could not be trusted. The plan worked and business boomed.

It was with this considerable experience of England and the friendly feeling that it had engendered that Maurois published in 1927 his first essay on Britain. He called it *Conseils à un jeune Français partant pour l'Angleterre.* The light and humorous touch displayed in this essay, which was couched in the form of a letter, is as delightful as it is surprising. During the post-war period England and France had seemingly forgotten their wartime comradeship and their common victory, and were indulging in recriminations and expressions of mutual distrust. The appearance of Maurois' charming and friendly little piece was therefore most helpful. Its chief virtue, aside from its wit, lay in his ability to blast the common assumption that national differences are proofs of inferiority in the nation under observation. Instead, he takes pleasure in discovering and in calling attention to differences between his own country and Britain, and he concludes that beneath the surface of some of the British traits which Frenchmen find least intelligible are signs of true greatness. He tells his putative traveler to bear in mind that the English have no inferiority complex. They are quite indifferent to what foreigners think of them. Above all, the French visitor must remember that they are as human as he is. Under an appearance of indifference they have passions, vanities, and all the rest of the human emotions. If he remembers this, he may find them not only likeable but admirable. In English translation this essay enjoyed wide popularity in Britain. It was an extension of the gospel according to *Bramble,* and it came at an auspicious time, as the latter had done.

To this essay Maurois soon added two more, one intended, according to its title, to give advice to a young woman of quality on the occasion of her embarkation for England, the other for a diplomat setting out for a tour of duty in the French embassy in London. In all three essays his advice is: Be yourself. Avoid at all costs the French defect of wondering what a person means when he says something. In France the chances may be ten to one that he means exactly the opposite. In England the odds are reversed. The Englishman means what he says. Not only that, he can conceive of no earthly reason why he should refrain from doing so. He does not tell you what you want to hear but gives you his honest opinion.

Bright memories of his younger days also linked Maurois with England. He had spent his first vacation there when he took a month's vacation from the woolen mill, and in a personal memoir he describes the fun of dating English girls, his pleasure in the pastimes of the English summer like punting on the river, going to see the plays of Bennett and Shaw, and playing, fairly innocently, at being the gay dog. His second happy recollection is of a vicarious experience, that of a youthful reading of Kipling, who taught him, he says, a lesson quite the opposite of the one he had learned from Alain. The latter was a rebel against society. Kipling taught the lesson that leaders are necessary and that the penalty for bad leadership is severe and often fatal. It was Kipling, together with Balzac, who was Alain's favorite, who guided Maurois' steps when he first learned to write.

With the years England became a kind of second home. Oxford, the town and the university, he came to know well as he guided his fiancée about during her studies there. He acquired a fondness for the quads and the old buildings that surrounded them which never left him. Without visits to British libraries he could not have written his biographies of Shelley, Byron, Disraeli, and Alexander Fleming. Without protracted stays in or near London he could not have done his research on the times of Edward VII or his work on the history of England. He became personally acquainted with many of the older literary figures and with some of those of his own generation. He became acquainted with Maurice Baring, to whom he became greatly attached, and his sketch of him in *Destins exemplaires* is for this reason far less an objective biography than a personal memoir. It is filled with emotion at the thought of Baring's kindness, and a sense of loss at his death after years of atrocious suffering. The country and its people he will always cherish. Its literature became a frame of reference. When speaking or writing about a French author, Maurois is as likely to compare him with a British writer as with another Frenchman. The anecdotes and illustrations which abound in his writings, and which seem to come from a limitless store, are as likely to concern England as France. Always a cultural relativist, he never contrasts his own country with Britain to the detriment of the latter. He readily admits that the beginnings of his affinity for Britain had a personal basis. He relates that when he was first assigned to duty with a British unit, he was extremely shy, and that British reticence, which respected this shyness, was exactly to his taste. No one asked him questions, and he asked none. In time he found out that his British comrades were sentimental but ashamed of the fact, another trait that he shared with them. He preferred action to talk, and so did they. But the essential point was that he was not only disposed to like the British, he really did.

The prodigious success of *Bramble* brought Maurois a welcome fame while he was still a non-commissioned officer. He was sought out at his post by the British commander-in-chief, Sir Douglas Haig, who talked to him about Colonel Bramble. After the war such contacts multiplied. *Bramble's* reputation brought him an invitation to attend the annual Pontigny conference of writers, British and French, and it was there that he made friends with several men whom he already admired such as André Gide, Lytton Strachey, and Charles DuBos. *Bramble* also brought him a not unwelcome fame in England. While traveling there he was invited to dinners and celebrations in his honor. At these affairs he met a variety of persons, the list of whose names reads like an excerpt from the social register. And scattered among the socialites were fellow writers whose friendship he was to find both satisfying and helpful. This was heady stuff for the author of a mere one or two books, but if it did nothing else, it cemented his love for England and the English people.

In an early appraisal of Maurois, Georges Lemaître called attention to the fact that when Maurois wrote *Bramble* and the *Discours du docteur O'Grady*, he had a rather limited knowledge of Britain and the British. It was only after the concentrated study that was required for the biographies of Shelley, Byron, and Disraeli that he finally came to grips with the true British character and began to make a realistic appraisal of it. In *Bramble* he had but suspected the existence of such qualities as ruthlessness and determination beneath a mocking façade, talk of playing the game, and not showing one's emotions. His study of the character of Byron was a revelation, for in him he saw not merely an individual whose desire to escape convention led him to unhappiness, failure, and anti-social conduct, but also, astoundingly, a typical Englishman. He decided that he was not, as often supposed, an unEnglish character, but a man whose principal difference from his fellows was that he gave vent to impulses and emotions that many of his countrymen felt but succeeded in controlling. Further reading confirmed this diagnosis. He perceived that even Edward VII hid under a calm exterior some of the elements of rebellion that propelled Shelley and Byron into conflict with society. As for Disraeli his struggle with society was, as it were, built in. How could it have been otherwise? The Jew in British society had to fight or be submerged, and the outward conformity and dandyism of "Dizzy" were but a well-fitting and habitual cloak hiding an unbreakable determination to succeed. It had been this determination that made him prime minister, author, lion of society and financier.

Insights into the true nature of British character, it seems, were coming Maurois' way thick and fast as he wrote his successive volumes dealing with her great men and her society, and it is to be regretted that during the latter part of his career he had less to say about Great Britain. Even so he came to be considered in France an expert on all things British, a reputation that he found embarrassing since he was modestly aware, as his knowledge increased, how much there was yet to know. Still, he was at all stages in his career willing and even eager to explain Britain to his countrymen. In 1935 he yielded to a request by the publisher Flammarion for a contribution to a series of short informative books on foreign countries. He called his volume quite simply, *Les Anglais*. It is a brief, factual pamphlet of sixty-four pages which explains the British system of education, recreation, and politics and gives some suggestions regarding the national character and the organization of society. Regrettably, it is tiresome stuff. There is more in the *Conseils à jeune Français* in half the space. Still, it may be argued that schoolboys would not be likely to read the latter. More's the pity!

II *America without Menace*

Maurois' acquaintance with the United States came later in his career, in 1927 and after, but his interest in the country and his fondness for it were to be deep and lasting. It was on the invitation of Princeton University that he made his first ocean crossing, a voyage that was to bring him for the first time into the classroom as a regular lecturer. He found the role quite different from that of occasional speaker or performer on the commercial lecture circuit, but he enjoyed it from the first and says that he found in it a second vocation. Nevertheless, student of Anglo-Saxon culture that he was, Maurois had certain hesitations before leaving home. Reports on the United States by French and English friends and observers were far from uniformly favorable. Americans themselves in their novels and plays seemed to be belatedly trying to outdo Zola in the violence of their denunciation of American society and its cultural aridity. H. L.

Mencken made sport of democracy. Scott Fitzgerald depicted the immorality of gilded youth. Politically the country was in the era of Coolidge and Harding. Fortunately for Maurois he did not intend to make a whirlwind tour from coast to coast or from border to border. His itinerary called for a protracted stay in the rather idyllic situation of Princeton, located in one of the best of small towns and quite removed from the hustle and bustle of the nearby cities. Once installed on campus, Maurois found himself surrounded by intelligent and cultivated people and in an atmosphere that contrasted radically with the quick-lunch, subway-rush kind of atmosphere that he had been led to expect. He was at once enchanted. If he had had doubts, they vanished, and there is nothing in anything that he has written about his first visit to justify his biographer Jacques Suffel in talking as follows about his first contact with America:

He was first astonished, not charmed. The noise deafened him, the size of the buildings overwhelmed him. Was this immense and motley nation a people of giants or a people of overgrown children? The movement of Paris seemed slight compared with that of New York. The metropolis, with its omnipresent advertising, its automobiles, its elevators and its telephones depressed the European. Was the Stars and Stripes to dominate the world?[60]

This is, I regret to say, the kind of malicious and ignorant nonsense that observers from a distance had been writing for years. It is particularly distasteful in this instance for it finds no warrant in Maurois' work. It was, of course, true that American critics of their country had found their counterpart in hostile European visitors. *Scènes de la vie future* was yet to be written, but its forerunners already existed. Thus the climate of opinion regarding the United States was so unfavorable that when Maurois reported his findings: that there was decency, intellectuality, and many another good quality to be found in the United States, just as they were to be found elsewhere, the interviewer from the *Nouvelles littéraires*[61] was not disposed to take his praise of the country seriously. His article, "Voyageurs d'hier et d'aujourd'hui," labeled Maurois and his book "perhaps not very brilliant . . . but useful and agreeable," implying in the same article that a less tolerant observer would have found a lot more to dislike. Such was the penalty for expressing an opinion counter to the established cliché that America was a horrible place. The three months that Maurois spent in the United States on his first visit were to make of him a lifelong champion of America and things American. He had no wish to write a hasty condemnatory tract, as vicious as it is misleading, repeating with eyes closed all the untruths he had learned before arrival and making no fresh observations of his own. Far from it. Still his pen could not remain idle. He wrote about his visit to America in the book *L'Amérique inattendue* (1931), which is mainly an account of his observations on a college campus. He sensibly restricted his remarks to the side of America that he had come to know, and he was pleased to be able to report to his French and English friends that scholarship was far from nonexistent in American universities, and that her students were willing and intelligent, as well as decent and well trained. The praise was warm, but the range of his knowledge was limited. Thus Maurois' modest aim and the modest conclusions of his book were but a slight antidote to the sort of anti-American propaganda which condemned America practically *in toto*.

Maurois' first visit was followed by a second in which he was accompanied by his wife, and from which a second commentary resulted, *En Amérique* (1933). More travel on Maurois' part enabled this book to have a wider scope than its predecessor, and this time he tried to do a bit of theorizing. By digging into the American past, he sought to interpret the present. He thought that he had found three spectres that haunt the American present: the Puritan, the pioneer, and the feudal lord. Each had his part to play in the conquest of the continent: the first by setting the moral tone and determining the attitude toward life which was to accompany the taming of the wilderness; the second by looking ever toward the new, the untried, and the unknown; and the third by his determination to master both men and materials in order to mold a new economy. Each in his way determined the direction that America was to take; each in his way still haunts America, though the situation that called forth his talents has long since passed. With these three stereotypes—and Maurois readily admits that they are no more than that—he thought he could understand the United States better then merely by poking his nose into slums or by visiting slaughterhouses. His mention of the latter establishments was undoubtedly in response to Duhamel's harsh remarks about his visit to those of Chicago. But not content merely to comment on the dubious value of such a visit, Maurois adjures the French visitor to go and see French slaughterhouses before talking about those of the United States. The former, he says, are less publicized and less hygienic.

A few years later, Maurois was to recall his advice to a young Frenchman about to visit England, and in the same spirit he wrote a companion essay with the title *Conseils à un jeune Français partant pour les Etats-Unis* (1947). In it he proffers this sage advice:

Since you have been preparing for your trip you have read a hundred books on America: forget them. The traveler, when he describes a far off country is likely to exaggerate its strangeness. As for me who am not trying to please you but to instruct you, let me tell you that the beings with a human countenance whom you will meet on the opposite shore after six days on the ocean, are not as different as you think from your friends in Europe or yourself. They are men who, like us, work, suffer, eat, drink, make love, read the poets, build temples and destroy them, are born and die. You are leaving for America, not the moon. Be simple.[62]

Maurois' third visit was of a different sort. He wished to see for himself the America of the depression years and to describe it for the French people. He had heard rumors in Europe to the effect that the economic difficulties in America were greatly exaggerated. It was even said that only the bankers were in trouble while the rank and file of Americans were doing business as usual. To get the facts, Maurois decided to travel widely throughout the states, to visit factories and flophouses, soup kitchens and welfare agencies. He also used his standing and influence to obtain interviews with leaders in government and industry. He talked to New Dealers Rexford Tugwell, Harry Hopkins, and General Hugh Johnson, the head of the National Recovery Administration. He studied the efforts of President Roosevelt to find a way out, and when he reached home he offered the public an accurate report in a book called *Chantiers américains* (1933). Shortly thereafter he took time out to describe college life in America and to appraise it favorably in *La Machine à lire les pensées* (1937), as we have already seen.

Maurois' fourth and least pleasant trip was to result in much frustration, and this frustration he recalls in the book entitled *Etats-Unis, 1939*. The Europe which Maurois had left behind him was on the verge of war. Hitler and Mussolini were rattling their sabres. American tourists, visiting Germany by the thousands, were being lectured about the inequities of the Treaty of Versailles. In Italy, incredible as it may seem, still other American tourists were overlooking the brutalities of fascism and choosing only to remember that "Mussolini made the trains run on time." In the United States the Communist party was making the most of the late depression.

In France and England politicians squabbled and temporized while Germany rearmed at a furious pace. Frenchman hated Frenchman. Englishman was suspicious of Englishman, and all of them had a grudge against the United States. It was the fashion, says Maurois, to blame the United States for all the evils on the planet, and evils were not lacking. "I found out very quickly," he says, "that this attitude was unjust. There is nothing more ridiculous than to blame the Americans for not being good Englishmen or good Europeans." [63]

Such was the sorry state of Maurois' world at the time of his trip to the United States. Once again he traveled far and wide, farther from the Atlantic seaboard than he had been before, and the farther from France he got, the worse, from his point of view was the atmosphere. In Washington he met President Roosevelt whose realism impressed him, but his travels outside the national capital showed how little the President's pro-European thinking was shared by the American people as a whole. Quarrels on the continent seemed terribly remote to farmers in Iowa and Texas, and to factory workers in Kansas City and Los Angeles. Even the intellectuals were disillusioned. They thought with some justice that England and France were handling international affairs badly, and in reply to Maurois' warning about the dangers inherent in German and Italian belligerence, they said in effect that matters could not be so bad as painted or France and England would stop their internal and external bickering long enough to prepare for the inevitable. Maurois spared no pains to report frankly at home on these sentiments. He warned his countrymen that railing against American attitudes would not change them, and told them flatly that if war came, America would not leap to her guns. He was as discouraged as he had ever been, and he said so. After his return home, in a shorter time even than he had feared or foreseen, he found himself in the army. The war had come.

III Asylum in the United States

When the phony war ended in blitzkrieg and a French defeat, Maurois, as we have seen, made a brief trip to England to talk to influential English friends and to broadcast to the British public on behalf of a prostrate and defeated France. But in those dark days he never lost faith in the part to be played by Britain and America. He preached steadfastness and courage in the face of defeat, and with General De Gaulle he stood practically alone as the prophet of a new France which would rise from the ashes of the old. As he was duty bound to do, he returned to France, was discharged from the army, and was given formal permission to go to the United States for an indefinite period. His immediate official reason was a commitment to give the Lowell Lectures in Boston. Once safe from the Nazis, his thoughts were mainly of his country, and he was to devote his time and energy to explaining her plight to American audiences. But this was not all. On his arrival in the United States in 1940, Maurois knew that he was embarking on no three-months lectureship, but he could hardly have foreseen that he was to remain on American soil for four long years. Or that during that time he was to become American in understanding and sympathy in a way that he would not have dreamed possible before the war. His pen provided him with a livelihood which he supplemented from time to time by a lectureship in one or another of the universities. He became a member of the Book-of-the-Month-Club jury and gave that most American of institutions the benefit of his excellent taste and wide reading.

Maurois' record of his thoughts and impressions during the period of exile are found in a number of places but notably in *Pages de mon journal, 1946* (American title: *From My Journal, 1946*). Obviously what had begun in the bitterness of exile turned into a happy and useful interlude in his life. He made himself a member of the American community and he was able to lead an active and busy life. But his most enjoyable period seems to have been that of his six-months lectureship at the new University of Kansas City, followed by a stay at Mills College in California. In Kansas City, Dr. Decker, the president of the university, became his good friend as did Henry Haskell, the dean of the college. He was also friendly with another famous American, William Allen White, with whom he worked on the book-club jury and who was his near neighbor in Kansas. He became acquainted with a number of small towns, for on his lecture tours he did not try to avoid engagements at the less important places. The fruit of these travels was that he came to know America well and came close to the American spirit. Only a sense of duty took him back to France where he felt that he must take part in the end of the conflict and use his pen and voice in the reconstruction of France after the defeat of the Nazis. Without this sense of urgency he might have remained in the United States, for he confessed that of all the places he had ever seen, California was, next to France, his favorite spot.

As usual, there were reviewers who did not find Maurois' latest book excellent. The reviewer of *The New Yorker* had this to say of the journal: "The author's observations on life in the United States are unusually benign, but, unfortunately, too often flat and superficial. The latter part of the journal, which deals with postwar France, has more sting and point, but not much." [64]

Maurois' next visit to American shores in 1948, two years after his happy return to France, was once more in the form of a lecture tour. Characteristically he did not shrink from visits to places not usually visited by Frenchmen. In addition to the inevitable New York and Princeton, plus fashionable Duke University, he lectured in Terre Haute, Indiana, in Oklahoma and in Kansas City, his old stamping ground. His casual contacts were rewarding as usual. He talked and read incessantly throughout his journey, and he ended his visit with an interview with President Eisenhower of Columbia University. As usual, he enjoyed himself hugely.

Maurois' methods of observation on all his travels in the United States were well calculated to make him a competent and reliable student of American culture. His most useful tool was the English language which he spoke and wrote with ease, but not without accent, as he himself said. This meant that he was not dependent on the French colonies or the Francophiles of the larger cities for his information. He read widely in Americana of all periods, and if he ever had any prejudices, they disappeared before his growing fund of information. The question-and-answer periods which he encouraged after his lectures called his attention to aspects of French life that Americans were uninformed about. They also revealed to him the ways of thinking of the American public. Such exchanges of ideas were of inestimable value. But even this public, by the very fact that it turned out to hear a French lecturer, might not be typical, and so Maurois used other resources to reach the common man. He was forever starting conversations with his seatmates on trains, planes, and buses. He talked to soldiers and sailors, to candy vendors, conductors and stewardesses, and the result was a detailed knowledge of the United States that has hardly been excelled by any other foreign visitor.

The tolerance and broadmindedness that were the by-products of his methods might have had dire consequences for Maurois at home if they had not been accompanied at all times by his equally sincere and outspoken love of his own country. But even patriotism could not keep him from irritating his own countrymen occasionally. As he talked about America, he sometimes paused to lecture Frenchmen on their failure to possess certain virtues which he admired in

America, like civic-mindedness, for instance. It is to be regretted that, except for the published journals, he never used in book form the detailed knowledge of the United States that he acquired. What he did by precept and example was to resist the malicious, the stupid, and the merely uninformed among his compatriots who used the United States in book and public lecture as a whipping boy for the world's ills. Such attitudes he could not tolerate. He remained a kind of apostle to the French, and his experience and background made him relatively immune from charges of venality and prejudice alike. He kept up his American contacts by repeated visits and he was and so considered himself, a friend of the Anglo-Saxon peoples.

IV *South America and Beyond*

Maurois' travels following World War II took him into other parts of the world. While protesting that travel took much of his time, he continued to move about. Indeed, it was obvious that he could not live without travel. Hardly had he set foot in France after the years of wartime absence than he set out on a trip to Switzerland, which he described as a country free from tensions and troubles. The following year he embarked on a lecture tour in Latin America. This trip is described in *Journal d'un tour en Amérique latine*. In his preface he repeats, but quite without irritation or sarcasm, a favorite Duhamelian theme: France will lose her cultural influence in Latin America unless she can export more of her classics in attractive and inexpensive editions. He observed that North American books were being read all through Latin America rather than French. He himself admitted that he knew little Spanish, and while he was ready to say a good word for the usefulness of English for all who live in the Western Hemisphere, he was nevertheless distressed to find so little interest in France and so little sale of French books. Quite without thinking about it, Maurois had assumed the truth of the French conviction that Latin America is a sphere of Gallic influence, and his astonishment to find a cosmopolitan civilization was therefore natural. With more time at his disposal he might have had something of value to say on the subject, especially since culture and cultural relativism were among his chief interests. What we have in this journal instead is a lucid but merely pleasant account of his first journey to the region, a journey from which was to come the novel *Les Roses de septembre* and the travel book on *Rio de Janeiro*. Still the journal is too brief and too hasty to deserve a significant place in his work.

In essaying Maurois' contribution to international amity and understanding, it must be recognized at the outset that he was practically alone in his day in his willingness to study Britain and the United States in a serious and unprejudiced manner. French travelers in the period between wars, oblivious to the very real defects of French life that existed beneath the surface, found it amusing and profitable to excoriate America for the faults, failures, and banalities which American critics were only too ready to join them in exposing. Britain, too, was the object of French suspicion. Meanwhile the British thought, quite mistakenly, as it later appeared, that the French were pursuing a needlessly anti-German policy, and all the excesses of National Socialist militarism and Hitlerian hatred of democracy could not shake them from their myopic view. The French returned the compliment in full measure with references to "perfidious Albion" and a conviction of British hypocrisy. Maurois' espousal of American causes was similarly heroic. Most French writers, even those who knew better, were content to drift with the tide. Maurois was not. The friendships of the years of World War I had demonstrated to him beyond a doubt the essential humanness of the British. He was to acquire a belief in the human qualities of Americans also. He was, in a word, to become a true cosmopolitan, and his contribution to international friendship must be an essential ingredient in any evaluation of his writing.

CHAPTER 8

A Niche in the Hall of Fame

FROM the inception of his literary career, beginning with the publication of *Les Silences du colonel Bramble,* Maurois acquired a following of his own, a group of enthusiasts for his writing who eagerly awaited the appearance of each new Maurois book and read it mainly to praise it extravagantly. Equally prominent on the literary horizon were a number of hostile critics who were willing to award him nothing more than an occasional sentence or two of grudging praise. But if the enthusiasms of the faithful were exaggerated on the one hand, so was the niggardliness of recognition. The productions of more than forty-five years of assiduous application to the art of writing in a variety of serious *genres* would appear to deserve more than the prejudice of extravagant praise or blame.

I *The Defects of His Qualities*

The majority of Maurois' outstanding qualities have been discussed in some detail in the foregoing pages. Less obvious are his failures and weaknesses. These, when examined minutely, have led at times to unwarranted conclusions regarding his work. It is alleged that he was lacking in many areas, as indeed he was. The fact is that Maurois, though he had ideas and a philosophy of life, was not primarily a thinker or philosopher. This means that he felt no need to expound or to develop a thesis in his writing. It means also that his books seldom became a vehicle for propaganda. It means that he was free to change his point of view without fear of presenting the public with an image of personal inconsistency. It means that in each of his successive novels and biographies he was free to examine some new aspect of life without having to make certain that each one fitted into a coherent philosophical pattern; that he need not, in a word, always say what was expected of him and nothing else. On the face of it, Maurois' refusal to be doctrinaire and to assume and maintain a rigid position ought to be regarded by public and critics alike as the sort of intellectual freedom required by a novelist if he is to do his best work and be creative. To do otherwise is to become the prisoner of a point of view. The doctrinaire writer may achieve greatness as a philosopher, but his work as a writer will be hampered, to say the least.

In our time few writers have been able to achieve complete freedom to write as they please. As one examines the productions of the galaxy of great writers who were Maurois' contemporaries, it becomes apparent that each in his own way had a special point of view. If one takes the obvious example of Jean-Paul Sartre, it becomes obvious that for better or worse his work is what it is because it reflects inexorably the existentialist philosophy that he expounds. Closely examined, most of the major novelists, with the exception of Maurois, display the same fidelity to the framework of their ideas. Duhamel, Romains, Malraux, Mauriac, Martin du Gard, Gide even, are all prisoners of their philosophical mansions. Enemies of Maurois, pointing this out, have remarked with more hostility than truth that this is because the latter had no philosophical position worth defending. The fact is that for the generation of novelists to which he belonged it was the fashion to espouse a point of view early in life and then to adhere to it through thick and thin even if the result were a marked similarity among successive literary productions. In the sense that the word "philosophy" may be applied to Sartre, it is true, therefore, that Maurois had no philosophy. He had, on the other hand, and for this we may thank his admiration for Balzac, a number of ideas that he liked to talk about and an abundant fund of common sense, and these assets save him from errors of repetition which crept sometimes into the works of his illustrious contemporaries.

A summary of Maurois' political ideas requires no great space for its elucidation. His notions, he says, are simple:

We must hope that politics, following the example of science, will stop trying to know the ultimate and will be willing to respect the conventions (recognized as such) as long as they are useful. Against the myths of politics, anger is as foolish as would be a revolution against the ether or an uprising against the x-ray. The king of England is a myth but a useful myth and therefore venerable. The right of property is a fiction, it may even be permitted to think it outmoded, and to judge it useful. But it is comic to hate it, and childish to worship it. Science cannot live without hypotheses, nor human societies without images. A people destroys one set of conventions only to turn to the worship of another.[65]

In the jargon of our day, these sentiments make our author a liberal conservative. Certainly his statement will please neither reactionaries nor radicals.

Maurois' primary concern is with the individual. "To write a biography," he says, "is to affirm implicitly one's faith in the individual." [66] It is the individual, as president, as general, or as a humble member of society who finds an occasion to make history. This democratic belief in the value of the individual is, to him, a basic idea. This is the theme of his biographies and histories and many of his essays. A belief in the need for gradual change in order to avoid revolution is also one of his basic ideas.

There is no specific echo of these ideas in his works. The individual in the novels is seldom concerned with ideas *per se*. His problem is to find a *modus vivendi* with a member of the opposite sex in a given situation. The basic drives for status, for response, and for new experience frequently lead an individual into adulterous relationships, and the resulting strains on the family tie are a frequent theme of Maurois' novels. In fact, adultery becomes an oft-repeated and even tiresome ingredient therein. But Maurois is not ashamed of his frankness. He tells us with some amusement how his revered master Alain, when visited by an inspector of public instruction, was in the process of explaining to his boys their duty toward prostitutes, and how he continued his exposition, ignoring the visitor's presence. Maurois says frankly that illicit sexual experiences were to be found in the background of most young men of his generation, and although he nowhere condones extra-marital experience or adultery, he admits that these two phenomena were very much a part of the pattern of life in Europe as most people lived it. He was, therefore, not wandering away from reality when he used adultery and its unhappy consequences as a frequent theme of his novels.

In his autobiography, Maurois speaks of his warm admiration for coeducation in America, where for the first time he observed the possibility of a different and better relation between young men and women. But whether within the framework of marriage or before, as in courtship, the problems of love are one of Maurois' recurrent themes. None of his heroes solves his problem in the same way as any other. Some make fools of themselves and ruin their lives for an ephemeral love affair. But Maurois points no lesson and draws no moral as such. His technique is more subtle. If he comes perilously close to moralizing by demonstrating through his characters that the wages of sin are, if not death, as least desperate unhappiness, he never actually does so. With but few exceptions neither does he permit his characters to live by or to express an amoral point of view. If they sin, they may be punished, but he avoids rewarding all good characters and punishing all bad ones. Still, he clearly implies that what is wrong is wrong, and this remnant of puritanism is enough to damn him with some readers.

Maurois carefully refrains in the biographies, even by implication, from hinting at personal disapproval of the sometimes atrocious conduct of his subjects. Byron, Hugo, George Sand, and Chateaubriand were, from the point of conventional morality, whether in America or Europe, shocking examples of persons who scorned the opinions of their contemporaries, but Maurois assumes, and rightly so, that it is the biographer's role not to castigate his subject but to represent him whole and without apology. This he does. Yet many of the critics regard Maurois as a moralist. He himself gives the following definition: "A moralist is not an author who gives lessons in morality, he is an author who deals with morals and manners." [67] True. Yet even in the narrower sense of being aware of the importance of morality in a society, Maurois is a moralist. He does not believe that man can live without a government, and he is far more convinced than his mentor Alain of the need for controls. He applies this attitude to marriage, to civic duty, and to the relations between nations. Without some sense of morality he feels that society is impossible. No book by Maurois, therefore, is without some hint of the concept of duty, unpreached but implicit in everything he writes.

Yet a deep conviction of the need for rules between individuals as well as between nations has never been an excuse for creating characters who are merely puppets. Maurois has created some unforgettable characters. The readers of *Climats* do not soon forget either Phillipe or Isabelle, and the readers of *Cercle de famille* are long haunted by the presence of the weak and pathetic Denise Herpain. Bernard Quesnay reminds us, as he was probably meant to do, of the young Maurois. In fact it has been said by some critics that all Maurois' characters are too plainly himself in his various moods and aspects, and at various times of his life. He himself agrees that this is so but asks: Where's the harm? If it be true that each of us has in him the stuff of several characters of fiction, what objection can there be to making use of the fact? Balzac used many sides of his own personality, and Maurois tells us not once, but repeatedly, of his admiration for him. Actually there is little actual borrowing from the nineteenth-century master. There could not be. Maurois would agree with those who maintain that in this day and age our understanding of human psychology and character has progressed sufficiently to make an application of Balzac's methods obsolete. Maurois does not commit the blunder of a blind imitation of Balzac. He does not, for instance, attribute to his characters a master passion. His men and women are of their time, with the psychological nuances of the twentieth century.

II *Persons and Plots*

Plot, with Maurois, is decidedly secondary in importance, as secondary as it was with Anatole France. His plots in most instances can be reduced to a sentence. *Bernard Quesnay:* the reluctant participant in the management of a woolen mill becomes progressively absorbed in its workings to the point of neglecting everything else. *Climats:* the jealous, overly loving and protective husband of Odile loses her thereby, and then finds out when married to Isabelle what it is like to be overly loved and protected. *Cercle de famille:* Denise Herpain, made unhappy because of her mother's infidelity, renders her own family unhappy by a repetition of the same sort of conduct. This is not to imply that for lack of plot Maurois' novels are also lacking in substance or fail to hold a reader's interest. But when they are compared with those of Roger Martin de Gard, Jules Romains, or even François Mauriac and Georges Duhamel, it becomes apparent that Maurois has built his character studies on a very slight framework of plot. Character and not plot is important to him. His leading characters are carefully delineated, while the least important one may be worked out in a long passage or may be tossed before the reader in a brief thumbnail sketch. The plots usually seem as if a minimum of effort had been expended upon them.

Of equal importance with character is what Maurois calls "climate," or atmosphere. In the novel of that name he has carefully explained what he means. Climate is the peculiar aura, atmosphere, or landscape that surrounds a person or group of persons. There was a Marcenat climate, an Odile climate, and an Isabelle climate. Climate is everywhere present. In his biographies as well as in his fiction his purpose is to feel and understand this climate for himself and then to recreate it for his readers. If he fails in this, he deems the book a failure. It was, in essence, the lack of a definable climate that made *Ni ange, ni bête* so unsatisfactory. Climate contributes indefinable charm that friendly critics claim to find in Maurois' books whether fiction, biography, or whatever. He possesses a skill all his own for creating climates, and a rapid review of his biographies easily demonstrates this fact. *Ariel,* though a special case, won its readers by its climate. But the same is true for Hugo, Dumas, Fleming, Madame de Lafayette, and the successive novels. Each has its climate.

Attempts to explain this special quality of Maurois' writing have been unsuccessful. Perhaps its secret lies in the fact that although Maurois is unfailingly objective in his treatment of his subject, he is never impersonal. And as he has a warm and outgoing personality himself, he manages to communicate some of his warmth to the characters about whom that he writes, whether they be real or imaginary. At times this warmth of climate becomes, especially in the books he wrote for children, a kind of *bonhomie* which Anglo-Saxons call "folksiness." Since this is hardly a French quality, it may account for the hostility of one recent French critic who remraks with a churlishness born of incomprehension that Maurois seems to be liked abroad, goodness knows why.[68] It is true, of course, that whimsy and folksiness are more appreciated by the British and Americans than by the French. The latter are likely to dismiss these qualities as sentimentality. Yet in his short biographical sketch of Dickens, Maurois repudiates Dickens' sentimentality as emphatically as any of his compatriots. The question may then be asked whether he indulges in its unconsciously. The answer should be no. Whimsy he uses, as well as affection and sympathy, but he seldom if ever drops into sentimentality. His characters are sometimes guilty of it to be sure, but the novelist always distinguishes carefully between their feelings and his own.

Maurois is quite adept in the use of another hardy French quality, that is humor as distinguished from the French *esprit,* or wit. His humor is best observed in his novels of fantasy and satire and in his works for children. There is also a great deal of irony on display in both *La Machine à lire les pensées* and *Le Peseur des âmes,* and irony the French both practice and preach. Humor, the producer sometimes of visceral laughter, the laughter devoid of cruelty, is little practiced in contemporary France, although Rabelais was one of its greatest practitioners. This, too, may account for Maurois' secondary popularity with French critics.

III *Unsolved Problems*

André Maurois was a Jew, a statement that ought to be irrelevant
in an enlightened society. But it is not irrelevant, a fact that Maurois
acknowledged by discussing its implications on several occasions.
His best thoughts on the matter are those which he penned with
regard to the biography of Disraeli. In an introduction included in
the collected works, he answers a critic who wants to know whether
his treatment of Disraeli was at all influenced by the fact that both
subject and biographer were Jews. He replies in the negative, but
goes on to say that the fact that Disraeli was a Jew did influence
him in his choice of a subject. He found out that his ideas and those
of the English statesman coincided on the role of the Jew in modern
society. Disraeli wished to help his fellow Jews to level all ghettos
and to achieve political and religious freedom. He succeeded in
doing this, but he did not seek to achieve privileges or equality for
the Jews *as* Jews. He did what he did because he held the conviction
that Jews, like every other alien, should disappear and become in-
distinguishable from other Englishmen. He repudiated Zionism and
its implications, and to prove the depth of his own convictions on
the subject he joined the Church of England. For many fellow Jews
this was a betrayal. For Disraeli it was a patriotic act and an act of
common sense. In addition to referring to the place of the Jew in
society, in connection with his biography of Disraeli, Maurois took
the occasion to talk about it again in a discussion of Duhamel's
Chronique des Pasquier. He says that the creation of the character
Justin Weill is one of the finest expositions of the problem that he
has ever read. At the same time he dismisses the detailed analysis
of Romain Rolland in *Jean Christophe* as totally unrealistic. The
question is no obsession with him, however, and he has never used
the problems of Jewish people as a theme for a novel.

Of far more concern to Maurois than the problems of minorities
is the fate of the modern nation as a whole. War, as one of the great
unsolved problems, he could not avoid, but instead of propagandiz-
ing against it directly, he saw it as a fact of life and treated it as
such. In his own life his conduct has been that of the citizen who,
however much he deplores the existence of a conflict, is ready to don
a uniform if called upon to do so. This, for doctrinaire pacifists, is
intolerable. Their contention is that so long as intellectuals are willing to fight, we will never put an end to war; wherefore the call to
protest and a refusal to fight. Maurois was too realistic to believe

that enough persons will adopt such a point of view in time to make it effective against a given threat of war. He pointed out that the unwillingness of the French to fight in 1939 led to their rapid defeat by the Germans and to the belated realization that occupation with its brutalities could be far worse than the war they wished to avoid. Maurois' writings, therefore, do not carry an anti-war message in so many words, but always implicit in them is the conviction that war is useless, inhuman, and must be done away with. He regarded world understanding as a slow but effective means of overcoming war, and for such understanding he worked hard. His attempts to depict the Anglo-Saxon cultures in a favorable light in his own country and his attempts in America and Britain to testify in behalf of the values of French culture are the tangible evidence of his relativism. He firmly believed that what one nation regards as standard procedure is almost sure to be regarded as odd or amusing by the people of another nation. In point of fact, he felt that there was no reason to assume the validity of one's customs or one's point of view. Look beneath the customs, we have heard him saying; the people you will find are not very different from yourself. Mankind is one. Superficial differences must not divide us. They will not do so unless we make the fatal blunder of assuming our own superiority.

Maurois refused, to some persons' annoyance, to allow himself to be drawn into the polemic against communism. It is plain that he was no Communist himself. He joined no Communist front organizations. He did not sign manifestoes or take part in leftist rallies. He quietly stated his opposition to communism, but he did not think it necessary to prove his patriotism by denouncing the Soviet Union. Since he regarded the denunciation of cultures other than one's own as frivolous, if not downright dangerous to peace and amity, so he thought that denunciations of Communist Russia served no useful purpose. Hitler was another matter, and Maurois, before World War II, frequently denounced the threat of National Socialism in violent terms. Maurois was a convinced believer in the virtues of capitalism as opposed to any other known system of economic organization. This is not surprising in view of his own experience as a former mill manager, for unlike many of his fellow authors who theorize for or against the current economic system, Maurois almost alone was qualified to speak as one who had defended the ramparts. Still he knew capitalism's defects, recognized the need for a balance between capital and labor and the need for social control to overcome the abuses of both sides. Such awareness kept him from attacking, as

others have done, all governmental attempts in France and elsewhere to influence the course of economic events. For him, economic
problems were not simple. For those who would understand something of their complexity he provided an excellent treatise on management and labor in *Bernard Quesnay*. Thus, although Maurois was
no socialist, he was fully aware of the basic issues with which
socialism, laissez-faire, and government control are concerned, and,
as usual, his approach was that of trying to understand rather than
to propose easy solutions.

IV   A *"Dangerous Facility"*

As Maurois observed again and again, he owed the general direction of his career to the influence of his teacher Alain, and he credits
him also with filling in some of the details. Alain observed in his
young student a tremendous energy, a considerable talent, and a
desire to excel. He feared that teaching would not provide a sufficient
outlet for these qualities. Above all, he was afraid that Maurois
would assume that he knew more about life than he actually did
and that he would be tempted to write novels without any solid,
personal knowledge of life's struggles. Go back to the factory, he
said. You need the kind of education you will get there. If your vocation for writing is real, you will come back to it. Meanwhile you
will learn something about human nature. This was undoubtedly
good advice. He also told Maurois that he noted in him a "dangerous
facility" which might lead to his becoming a superficial writer.

Looking at the immensity of Maurois' production, critics might
have said that Alain was right. Maurois has been accused again and
again of doing too much too fast. The extent of his work—much of
it, like the histories and biographies, based upon arduous and in-
escapable hours in the library—has caused the envious to complain.
He was even accused of being a rich dilettante whose income after
his first successes, added to what came to him from his share in the
family business, was such that he could spend prodigious sums on
secretarial help. He was accused of turning over all his basic research
to assistants, reserving for himself the pleasanter and more creative
task of putting the materials together after the hard, the unrewarding, and the disagreeable work in the library had already been done
for him. This he denied categorically. He declared that with the
exception of typing, a skill which he did not possess, and which his
wife did cheerfully and well for him, he did all his own work. Such
a statement should satisfy all but the most skeptical. How, then, it

is asked, could Maurois accomplish the manifold, the complex, the multifarious tasks that he took upon himself? His production is vast. Can all his achievements be laid at the door of the dangerous facility of which Alain warned him? Maurois will not let us believe it. He says that he does not write easily, and from his remarks on the subject it is easy to see that he was not a little irritated to hear it assumed that his "easy style" was the product of natural talent. He says on the subject:

. . . "an easy, limpid and crystal clear style," they say. But that style, for better or worse was a conquest. If ever some scholar, struggling with a thesis, studies one of my discarded scraps, he will be astonished to find ten, twenty, successive versions of each sentence. A word is chosen, crossed out, replaced, crossed out again, and thus endlessly. Adjectives are deleted, precious expressions are condemned and pedantries eliminated. What is the object of this incessant labor? To satisfy a potent instinct which makes me look for transparency, the final touch and above all a total agreement between the word and the thing.[69]

This statement should do much to erase the image of the rapid and superficial writer that has sometimes been conjured up. It should replace that image with a perfectionist whose stylistic success is, like the accuracy of his histories and biographies, intimately related to the extent of the effort and conscientiousness that he applied. Undoubtedly, since practice makes perfect, Maurois was able as a mature writer to obtain his effects, stylistic and otherwise, with less expenditure of effort than was necessary in the early days; but if writing came easier to the man of middle age and beyond, he seemed to have regarded his release from some of the drudgery as but an incentive to take on more work. The result was that titles of books written by him have multiplied as fast as his indefatigable pen could write them.

Maurois' way of expressing himself, which we call "style," more than any other single ingredient in his writing has won him a steadfast following. His sentences, his phrases, his metaphors are a part of that style. Analysis of them is not very difficult. His stock of words is not unusual, nor is his syntax. As Pascal observed, the same ball is played by all the players in a tennis match, but some are more skillful than others and, therefore, more fun to watch than others as they play the game. So it is with Maurois. People have found him a pleasure to read. His ideas are easy to follow. His disarming simplicity makes complex subjects seem easy. He has discussed his method at some length in the autobiographical *Portrait d'un ami qui s'appelait moi* (1950), and there is little for criticism to add to what he says there:

> I simply try to say what I have to say and to preserve the movement of my thought. Most of my sentences are short. When I am lucky they become a part of a master musical phrase.[70]

He tells us that dialogues are the easiest kind of writing for him as he is accustomed to think in terms of pros and cons. An argument seldom occurs to him without setting in motion an inner dialogue in which he tests opposing arguments. This trick of style has puzzled many of his critics who are always wondering which of the two points of view presented are the author's own. Maurois' answer is that his thought is expressed by both sides.

V *The Pinnacle*

Election to the *Académie française* crowned Maurois' work in 1939 on the eve of World War II. But as Frenchmen and knowledgeable foreigners well know, election does not guarantee immortality. In fact, a literate Frenchman would be hard put at any given moment to name all the supposedly distinguished writers who are its members. "Distinguished" is a relative word. Not only Maurois but his critics have already asked how long the books that are contained in the *Oeuvres complètes* will continue to circulate widely in the libraries of Europe and America. The answer to this question will finally decide Maurois' place in literary annals. Only a tentative reply can be given at this point.

As already noted, Maurois' competition in the field of the novel is stiff. The first six and a half decades of this century have been a period remarkable in quantity, quality, and diversity. Maurois' bid for permanence must repose on two or three titles at most: *Bernard Quesnay, Climats* and perhaps *Cercle de famille. Bramble*, too, is sure to be remembered as part of the literature of World War I. Each of these works has qualities that will entitle it to honorable mention in the field of fiction. But Maurois' advocate will probably have to be content to see him assigned to second division in the field, for there are novels by contemporaries which surpass his own. He was not, nor can we expect him to be accounted, the outstanding novelist of his time.

In biography his stance is better. Not only did he become the outstanding biographer of France but of his time. He is virtually without competition in the breadth and solidity of his work. His only possible rival in the field was the late Emil Ludwig whose method is akin to his in its careful attention to detail and its attempt to tell its story interestingly and with enthusiasm; but there the parallel ends. Ludwig's *Beethoven* and *Napoleon* are ponderous beside the biographies of Maurois. The latter was a reader of Ludwig's books, and with his usual graciousness he paid tribute to his work at the time of his death. Maurois outstripped the German in popularity, and it was his influence largely that made biography a field for the general reader, enlarging its scope and elevating it from its previous unglamorous function as an adjunct to critical or scholarly research.

Maurois may be said to have created the market for biography in France and in the United States. After he began to write, new and forthcoming biographies became a focus of public interest no less than novels. In fact, the recent evolution of the novel into experimental forms has, to a considerable extent, driven the middle class away from fiction, and biography bids fair to replace it as enjoyable yet intellectual reading. Other biographers have joined the field since Maurois first began to write, and therefore the credit for the current popularity of biography cannot be laid at his doorstep alone; but the initial move was his, and much that followed was influenced by his style and his method.

In that method, whether in biography or in history, Maurois excels. Yet there have been unfavorable criticisms. His appeal is said to be that of an ephemeral magazine article. Maurois, it is alleged, never comes to grips with the really difficult problems that he encounters in the course of his biographical researches. It is further alleged that he glides over all that is sordid, since his chief desire is to provide easy reading for unthinking minds. These are the charges. How ridiculous they are can be realized by anyone who is even superficially acquainted with the lives of George Sand and Chateaubriand, to take but two examples. Sorting truth from fiction and distortion to tell their lives in a straightforward manner was a task of incredible difficulty, and a simple comparison of Maurois' biographies with those which preceded them should convince any honest skeptic that nothing is omitted and nothing is simplified to the detriment of the life story he is trying to tell. The same is true even for the biography of Shelley, for *Ariel*, despite its deceptive simplicity, is a work based solidly on scholarship. One has only to consider the accusation that Maurois based his work entirely on his reading of Dowden's solid but less readable biography to realize how absurd it is to accuse him of superficiality on the one hand while at the same time accusing him of plagiarizing the most scholarly of works for the benefit of his own. It would be fairer to say that if the subjects of Maurois' biographies seem human and accessible, it is because he made them so, and not because the material is intrinsically easy. We have only to read the productions of the "life and works" school of biography, to which Maurois alludes in his lectures on biography to see the differences between the lucid and penetrating manner of his writing and the tiresome collection of facts which passed for biography before his time. With Maurois, facts are used to illumine, and he proved that they are not intrinsically dull.

Much that has been said in praise of Maurois' biographies may also be said of his historical writing, although the sum total of his contribution to the field was less remarkable. But even in this field, in which we can claim for him only amateur status, he has made his mark. Not all the historians of our time have written well by any means, and with the increasing complexity of the world, or at least with our increasing awareness of its complexity, to have written lucid and intelligible history is by no means a negligible achievement. Maurois turned to writing history for the same reason that he wrote novels and biographies: to find solutions to problems that beset him. He wished to understand the Britain of which he was so fond. Similarly, at a later date, he wanted to understand America. Although he was well aware that adequate, even brilliant, histories were available in English, he did not find anything that quite suited him as history intended for a French audience. This he determined to provide. He has been widely read for his pains, though a few professional historians have found it hard to forgive him for taking the facts that have long been at their disposal and making the telling of them an art. This, in essence, is what he did.

VI *The Man Himself*

The question is asked why the writings of Maurois are always a pleasure to read. As we have seen, style is one answer. But style is not merely words. It is the man behind the words, as already suggested. Visitors to Maurois' home, even casual interviewers, agree that he was a delightful person to meet. He had none of the academician's stuffiness and none of the doddering conservatism of old age. He seemed alive, his mind keen, his interests broad. He liked to talk and to listen, and it is the ensemble of these qualities that he managed to convey to the printed page. The delightful conversationalist of the drawing room becomes in the novels the creator of delightful conversations. The attractive and winning manner of the lecture platform is transferred without loss of warmth to the printed page. His tongue did not stiffen when what he was about to say was conveyed by the hand instead. But it is not enough to say all this. A number of articulate speakers and writers win themselves no public at all, and this is probably because they are mainly interested in themselves. Maurois has the additional quality of sympathy for and interest in his fellow man. One seldom feels in the man or his work a suppressed desire to sneer, to be snobbish, or to turn his fellow into a duplicate of himself. As it is said of the best actors that they have the gift of making each person in an audience feel that their acting is performed for him alone, so it may be said of Maurois' writing that it seems to each reader as if it were directed toward him alone. He avoids coldness, is unafraid of enthusiasm, smiles and laughs with his characters, and suffers with the subjects of his biographies. What sort of man he was not even his autobiography can tell us, for from his books we create our own image of him. He appears to have been a man of simplicity, directness and frankness, whose chief interest was in his fellow man. This is the essence of his work, and this, if anything, is what will make his works live. Ideas, though he had plenty of them, are not his chief asset. Sartre or even Jules Romains can outpoint him in the domain of intellect. Georges Simenon uses more complicated plots in his novels than Maurois ever troubled to invent. Dowden's life of Shelley has a greater accumulation of erudition than Maurois aspired to, for into its ponderous tomes went a lifetime of study. But *Ariel*, in its way, is superior to Dowden just as *Climats* is superior to much of Simenon.

In the last analysis we must rest Maurois' case on his personality and his style, on his manner, not on his matter. His matter is very good. In biography it is even unique, but his style is his greatest asset and his outstanding quality. The "dangerous facility" of which Alain warned him was, in the final analysis, the priceless ingredient. Like Balzac, he came after much practice to write with apparent ease, and if, as he says, the final product is a repatched, reworked, rewritten jungle of confused sentences, this fact is not apparent to the reader. If he had used his natural facility without conscious art, he might have been led to judge the world and to write about it before acquiring much actual experience of it, as Alain feared. Fortunately, however, in writing, as in the mill, he was willing to work, and his talent was used to convey honest opinions honestly arrived at through long experience, hard work, and personal tragedies. One aspect of facility he did possess, and that was the gift of seeing people as they are. He learned to capture their attitudes and their intellectual profile with the knack of the portraitist in water color or pastel. He used this ability in all his work, but it was especially invaluable in the portrayal of characters in fiction or biography. Part of his facility, too, was a positive genius for perceiving the difference between the merely sensible and the doctrinaire approach to a problem, and he invariably chose the former.

His leading philosophical idea is the oneness of the human race and its need to find peaceful solutions for its differences. But international understanding is a large concept. For his contribution Maurois chose but a single facet of the problem. He always thought that much would be gained if Frenchmen and Anglo-Saxons could have a mutual respect and understanding based on the realization that the problems of the twentieth-century human being transcend such petty differences as national mores or local eating habits. But even this serious preoccupation was not permitted to become a tiresome leitmotif in his work. Humanity as a whole was more important to him than Franco-British or Franco-American rapprochement. In fact, humanity as a whole was vastly more important than its parts. Whether he was writing history, biography or fiction it was Maurois' humanness that is his outstanding quality. He was, moreover, a humanist with an active pen and a humanist with a sense of proportion. Little more than that would be needed to make him popular in the United States, for we, too, are humanists, and we have often suffered the slings and arrows of outrageous attacks.

Alone, or almost alone of his generation in Europe, Maurois found it possible to remain guardedly optimistic. "I do not believe," he said, "that life is an evil without a remedy." [71] Such moderate optimism, which is the accepted attitude in America, was irritating to many of his European colleagues, many of whom could very well be called "professional pessimists." And this is but another aspect of Maurois which endears him to the Anglo-Saxons and helps to alienate him from certain intellectual circles in his own country.

In an interview recorded in his book on Maurois, Jacques Suffel reports him as having answered the question of the why of human existence as follows:

We have tasks to perform. They are within the reach of our faculties and our strength. Let us perform them. What more do you want? It is not for us to ask why we are men. We are men. That's the way it is. Let us try to act our part.[72]

It is easy to attack such a philosophy as not sufficiently abstruse and therefore not worthy to be regarded as a philosophy at all. Indeed, one interviewer who heard Maurois begin to expound his ideas burst out with: "But that's simply Candide's philosophy which says that we must cultivate our garden." To which Maurois replied with simplicity, "Perhaps." [73] As regards human relations, he considered himself a moralist which, as we have seen, he equates with being a student of *moeurs*, or mores. And among the most important of our mores are our rules of conduct. For him there could be no sterile prohibitions designed to take the joy out of life. On the contrary, the rules society has made in its own behalf exist to facilitate the pursuit of happiness. Anarchy, he believed, is not a favorable climate for man.

Maurois was barely in mid-career when he became the subject of several excellent but perhaps premature evaluations. In 1931 his work was evaluated in two such books, one by the Belgian Justin Sauvenier (1932) and the other by the Englishman David Larg (1932). The latter wrote a witty and perceptive piece about Maurois that is as much an essay on modern literature, comparing English and French points of view, as it is an evaluation of Maurois. The work of Georges Lemaître, *André Maurois* (1939) is of a different sort. His approach is businesslike, and he proceeds at once to the heart of the matter. In addition to providing the usual biographical background offered by all the successive critics, he makes some solid contributions of his own. The most noteworthy of these, in view of the fact that his book appeared early in Maurois' career, is the idea that the works should be viewed as an organic whole. While others have found it difficult to reconcile the biographer with the novelist, or the essayist with the writer of fantasies, Lemaître thinks that all these activities are explainable in terms already furnished by the life of the author. Did not the latter say that even a biography can be written in answer to an inner need and to relieve oneself of the presence of an inner tension? Lemaître fancies that he sees in all Maurois' work an attempt to reconcile within himself the rebel that he tried to exorcise by writing about Shelley and Byron, the Jew whom he satisfied with the writing of *Disraeli,* the moralist and man of convention whom he reveals in *Climats* and *Cercle de famille,* and the conservative liberal of the historical writings in which revolutionaries are given their due and more. He also suggests, with perhaps somewhat less cogency, that each of Maurois' works corresponds to a particular period of his life. Thus *Bramble, Ni ange, ni bête,* and *Ariel* belong to the young Maurois who was struggling to find himself. *Climats* and the early novels reflect his first marriage and the conflict between ambition and duty. The later biographies and histories are seen as representing the happily married Maurois to whom honors and kudos have come in profusion. There is, of course, some merit in this suggestion, if it is not too rigidly applied. Maurois' evolution was bound to follow his personal life. The autobiographical strain is strong in him even though he has explained the kind of metamorphosis that must take place before personal experience becomes objective writing. Everything that he said and did are, after all, a product of Maurois the man, and if one avoids too doctrinaire an application of his biography, such comparisons can be useful.

As can easily be seen from the foregoing pages with their frequent references to critical opinions of Maurois' works which were expressed as they appeared, he was not spared critical comment and analysis through the years. Because he was a full-time practitioner of the craft of writing it was inevitable that his name should seldom have been absent from the review columns of France's many literary magazines. And because he wrote a great deal about England and America, he won himself a place in literary circles in both countries. His work has been translated into English rapidly and well, and he has been discussed almost as frequently in British and American periodicals as in those of his own country. The reading of a fair sample of the hundreds of reviews that have greeted his successive works make plain that he never lacked for evaluation, sympathetic or otherwise. A conspicious flaw in some critical reviews has been the tendency to review his minor works as if they were major ones and to find fault with them for their unpretentiousness. Thus one reviewer called his *Voltaire,* a modest work, not very profound. His *Tourgeniev* was called too brief. The fact that many of his short biographies had their origin either in magazine articles or in speeches was not taken into account. Maurois' point of view in this regard was logical. He lived by his pen and he saw no reason why short, unpretentious works should not be published, but he did not expect serious criticism to be leveled at him for failing to accomplish in popular articles what he did so well in his longer books. But he has been frequently castigated for lack of depth, hasty composition, or a failure to analyze properly the literary achievements of the subject of his biography. No allowance was made for the fact that the kind of sketch that he was presenting required neither more nor less space than he actually devoted to it. Yet his achievement in some of the short biographies is as worthy of praise as his achievement in the longer ones. To apply the same standards of criticism to the sketches in *Destins exemplaires* as to the monumental achievement of *Prométhée* or *Disraeli* is to be unrealistic. Yet this is but one of several forms that critical opinions have taken. Maurois generally declined to reply, although when specifically accused at one point of dishonesty, he rose in his wrath to defend himself, as we have seen. But he knew that to counterattack the critics is a thankless task. He preferred to cultivate his garden.

In short, the truth would seem to be that Maurois was capable of an enormous amount of work. He was indefatigable. If he had a fault, it has been an excessive willingness to discuss his work with reporters and writers of theses. He yielded too often to requests for an opinion or an article. He occasionally allowed minor stories and essays to be printed that might better have been left to future scholars to discover. Even so, it is noteworthy that in his collected works he deliberately left out many of his excellent critical articles as well as most of his casual contributions to periodicals. He appears to have been saying that these writings are not those by which he is willing to be judged. And it would seem only fair to concur with him. What he did include is a vast and varied work, and much of it deserves our attention and our unqualified praise.

Notes and References

A number of Maurois' briefer publications are out of print and therefore rare. All footnotes refer to the most readily available editions, especially the *Oeuvres complètes*, whenever possible.

1. Michel Droit, *André Maurois*, Paris: Editions universitaires, 1953, p. 119.
2. Edmond Jaloux, *Perspectives et personnages*, Paris: Plon, 1931, p. 240.
3. Daniel Mornet, *Histoire de la littérature et de la pensée contemporaines*, Paris: Larousse, 1946, p. 150.
4. *Can Our Civilization Be Saved?*, Philadelphia, Penna.: Brandeis Lawyers' Society, 1949, p. 17.
5. Paris: Emile-Paul Frères, 1927.
6. *Les Nouvelles littéraires*, March 18, 1948.
7. *Oeuvres complètes*, Paris: Grasset, 1950, X, 358.
8. Jacques Hameline, "Pourquoi avez-vous choisi le pseudonyme d'André Maurois?" *Nouvelles littéraires*, August 4, 1949.
9. New York: Harper and Bros., 1951.
10. *Mercure de France*, 155–156, 2 (May 15, 1922), 184–185.
11. Jacques Suffel, *André Maurois*, Paris: Flammarion, 1963, p. 37.
12. May 18, 1950.
13. *Oeuvres complètes*, I, iv.
14. *Ibid.*, I, 390.
15. *Nouvelle revue française*, 38 (April 1, 1932), 746.
16. Vol. 92, no. 4757 (May 5, 1934), 26.
17. *Oeuvres complètes*, V, 351.
18. *Les Nouvelles littéraires*, April 18, 1931.
19. *André Maurois*, Palo Alto, California: Stanford University Press, 1939, p. 99.
20. January 1, 1939, pp. 126–128.
21. *Portrait d'un ami qui s'appelait moi*, Namur, Belgium: Wesmael-Charlier, 1959, p. 46.
22. *Mes Amitiés spirituelles, André Maurois*, Brussels: Editions de la Belgique, 1932, p. 119.
23. "Alain et le romanesque," in *Robert et Elizabeth Browning, Portraits, suivis de quelques autres*, Paris: Grasset, 1955, p. 211.
24. *Oeuvres complètes*, IX, 4.
25. *Ibid.*, II, iii.
26. *Ibid.*, II, i.
27. *Ibid.*, XV, preface.
28. Jacques Suffel, *op. cit.*, p. 172.
29. Pierre Brodin, *Maître et témoins de l'entre deux guerres*, Montreal: Valiquette, 1943, p. 150.
30. April 18, 1931.
31. *Oeuvres complètes*, V, 3.
32. *Atlantic Monthly*, 201, 92 (March 1958), 550.
33. *Saturday Review of Literature*, 38 (Feb. 5, 1955), 12.
34. *New York Times Book Review*, May 22, 1966, 2450 w.
35. June 5, 1966, p. 3.
36. *Nouvelle revue française*, 49 (Sept. 1, 1937), 442.
37. *Oeuvres complètes*, XI, 1.
38. *If Louis XVI Had Had an Atom of Firmness*, London: Longmans, Green and Co., 1931.

39. *Oeuvres complètes*, III, IV–V.
40. Suffel, *op. cit.*, p. 118.
41. April 25, 1937, 1350. "Book Review," p. 3.
42. June 5, 1947.
43. *Oeuvres complètes*, III, iv.
44. Vol. 20, no. 239 (Dec. 1940), p. 287.
45. *Oeuvres complètes*, VIII, 335.
46. *Ibid.*, IX, 268.
47. Vol. 142, no. 179 (Jan. 15, 1936), p. 79.
48. *Saturday Review of Literature*, Vol. 13 (1935–1936), no. 7 (Dec. 14, 1935), p. 5.
49. *Introduction à la méthode de Paul Valéry*, Paris: Editions des cahiers libres, 1933. Before inclusion in the *Etudes Littéraires* this lecture had been separately published.
50. Suffel, *op. cit.*, p. 88.
51. *Saturday Review of Literature*, 33, II (June 3, 1950), 19.
52. *New York Herald Tribune Book Review* (April 16, 1950), p. 1500.
53. *Oeuvres complètes*, XV, 222.
54. Published in New York as *Living Thoughts of Voltaire*, Longmans, 1939.
55. *Oeuvres complètes*, XV, 224.
56. Didier, New York, 1944, p. 213.
57. Feb. 6, 1944, p. 550.
58. *Oeuvres complètes*, X, 129.
59. *Nouvelle revue française* (July 1, 1933), p. 144.
60. *Op. cit.*, p. 121.
61. March 10, 1934, p. 230.
62. *En Amérique*, Paris: Flammarion, 1933, p. 114.
63. Suffel, *op. cit.*, p. 128.
64. Vol. 23: IV (Feb. 7, 1948), 79.
65. *Oeuvres complètes*, V, 291–292.
66. *Ibid.*, V, iii.
67. Suffel, *op. cit.*, p. 163.
68. Marcel Giraud, *Guide illustré de la littérature française moderne*, Paris: Seghers, 1949, pp. 121–122.
69. Suffel, *op. cit.*, p. 18.
70. *Ibid.*, p. 107.
71. *Oeuvres complètes*, II, v.
72. Suffel, *op. cit.*, p. 196.
73. *Ibid.*, p. 195.

Selected Bibliography

INTRODUCTORY NOTE

In common with most European men of letters André Maurois' works are frequently published in small original editions, then republished as these are exhausted. He also had the custom, in which he was not alone, of changing his titles. By the addition or subtraction of a chapter or two, he made a somewhat different work from the original. The publication of the *Oeuvres complètes,* which began in 1950, has helped to straighten out some of the confusion. But no additional volumes have been published for more than ten years, and in the interim Maurois' pen has continued to be active. To add to the bibliographer's problems, he also chose to omit a number of books from the collective edition. Still, all his books, together with his prefaces and articles, are to be found in Talvart et Place, *Bibliographie des auteurs modernes de langue française, 1801–1958,* Vol. XIV, which is a safe and generally accurate guide. The student will also note that there have been collective editions of several kinds of works. The novels were published as *Romans* (Gallimard, 1961); the biographical works concerning British subjects as *L'Angleterre romantique;* the fantasies as *Les Mondes impossibles;* and the biographical fiction as *Les Mondes imaginaires.*

A list of translations into English of Maurois' major works is also given herein. For titles not listed, the Library of Congress Catalogue is an accurate and accessible guide. Maurois has been served by many translators among whom Hamish Miles and Gerard Hopkins are outstanding.

At the end of the bibliography are listed the books about Maurois that have been most helpful in the preparation of this study. Of special interest is the volume by Jacques Suffel, *André Maurois,* in which each chapter by Suffel is followed by a commentary written by Maurois in which he replies to what has been said about him.

For a guide to the numerous and mostly ephemeral articles that Maurois published in distinguished and undistinguished magazines while he was in the United States from 1940 to 1944, the reader is referred to the exhaustive list by Doxie Dexter in her unpublished master's thesis, "André Maurois, Conciliator" (University of Kentucky, 1946).

PRIMARY SOURCES

Adrienne, la vie de la marquise de La-fayette. Hachette, 1961.*

Alain. Editions Domat-Montchrétien, n.d. (1950).

* Place of publication is Paris unless otherwise noted.

A la recherche de Bramble, inédit, *Oeuvres complètes,* pp. 191–251.

A la recherche de Marcel Proust. Hachette, n. d. (1949).

L'Amérique inattendue. Editions Mornay, 1931. A collection of articles previously published in various periodicals.

Anarchie. Liège: Les Editions de la Lampe d'Alladin, 1926.

Les Anglais. Flammarion, 1935.

L'Anglaise et autres femmes. Nouvelle société d'éditions, 1932. Short stories later included in the collective volume *Toujours l'inattendu arrive.*

Arabesques. Chez Marcelle Lesage, 1925. Later incorporated into *Lyautey.*

Ariel, ou la vie de Shelley. Grasset, 1923.

Un Art de vivre. Plon, 1939.

Aspects de la biographie. Au Sans Pareil, 1928.

Aux innocents les mains pleines, proverbe en un acte. La Table Ronde, 1955.

Beethoven, "Le Mystère des amours," with Jules Romains, Robert d'Harcourt, Jacques Brenner, Bernard Gavoty, André Jolivet, Alfred Kern, Hermann Scherschen, Hachette, 1961.

Bernard Quesnay. Gallimard, 1926.

Biographie, Editions Estienne, 1957.

Les Bourgeois de Witzheim. Grasset, 1920.

Byron. Grasset, 1930.

Byron et les femmes. Flammarion, 1934.

Can Our Civilization Be Saved? Philadelphia, Penna.: Brandeis Lawyers' Society, 1949.

Une Carrière. Cité des livres, 1926.

Centenaire de la mort de Lamennais. St. Malo, 23 juillet, 1954, discours de M. André Maurois. Firmin-Didot, 1954.

Centenaire de la mort de Frédéric Chopin. au Château de Nohant, 24 juillet, 1947. Discours de M. André Maurois. Firmin-Didot, 1949.

Ce que je crois. Avec les objections faites par quelques lecteurs et les réponses à ces objections. Grasset, 1952.

Ce qu'on appelle charme. Claude Aveline, 1927.

Le Cercle de famille. Grasset, 1932.

Chantiers américains. Gallimard, 1933.

Le Chapitre suivant. Simon Kra, 1927.

Chateaubriand. Grasset, 1938.

Chefs-d'oeuvre des aquarellistes anglais. Turner et ses contemporains. Texte d'André Maurois. Introduction de Laurence Binger. Plon, 1939.

Choses Nues. Gallimard, 1963.

A Civil War Album of Paintings by the Prince de Joinville. New York: Atheneum, 1964.

Climats. Grasset, 1928.

Conseils à un jeune Français partant pour l'Angleterre, suivis d'une *Lettre à une jeune femme de qualité partant pour Londres au moment de la "saison,"* et de *Notes pour un homme d'état française qui traverse pour la première fois la Manche.* Grasset, 1938.

Conseils à un jeune Français partant pour les Etats-Unis. Editions de la Jeune Parque, 1947.

Contact (Premières impressions d'Amerique). Maestricht: Stols, 1928.

La Conversation. Hachette, 1927.

Le Côté de Chelsea. Gallimard, 1932.

Cours de bonheur conjugal. Hachette, 1951.

J. L. David. Editions du dimanche, 1948.

Décors. Emile-Paul, 1927.

De la Bruyère à Proust. Fayard, 1964. These essays and several others have been reprinted under various titles, e.g., *Etudes littéraires,* q. v.

De Proust à Camus. Perrin, 1963.

Les Derniers jours de Pompéi. Papine, 1928. Incorporated into *Les Mondes imaginaires.*

Destins exemplaires. Plon, 1952.

Deux fragments d'une histoire universelle 1992. Editions des Portiques, 1928.

Les Deux Géants, histoire parallèle. Les Etats-Unis, André Maurois. Le URSS, Louis Aragon. Editions du Port-Royal, 1964, 5 vols.

Dialogues des vivants. Fayard, 1959.

Dialogues sur le commandement. Grasset, 1924.

Le Dîner sous les marroniers, Contes et nouvelles. Editions des Deux-Rives, 1951.

La Malédiction de l'or. Editions des Deux-Rives, 1951.

Discours de réception de M. André Maurois à l'Académie française et réponse de M. André Chevrillon. Grasset, 1939.

Discours de réception de M. Jean Cocteau à l'Académie française et réponse de M. André Maurois. Gallimard, 1955.

Les Discours du docteur O'Grady. Grasset, 1922.

Edouard VII et son temps. Editions de France, 1933.

Eisenhower. Didier, 1945.

En Amérique. Flammarion, 1933.

Espoirs et souvenirs. New York: Editions de la Maison française, 1943.

Un Essai sur Dickens. Grasset, 1927. Also published as *Dickens.* Ferenczi et fils, 1935.

Etats-Unis 39. Journal d'un voyage en Amérique. Editions de la France, 1939.

Etudes américaines. New York: Editions de la Maison française, Essays and articles published in the newspaper *Pour la Victoire,* 1944–1945.

Etudes anglaises. Grasset, 1927.

Etudes littéraires. Editions Sfelt, 1947, 2 vols.

Femmes de Paris. Plon, 1954.

Fragment d'un journal de vacances, Angleterre, 1928. Emile Hazan, 1929. Incorporated into *Mes Songes que voici.*

La France change de visage. Gallimard, 1956.

Franklin, la vie d'un optimiste. Didier, 1945.

Frédéric Chopin. Montreal: Editions variétés, 1942.

Grands écrivains du demi-siècle. Club du livre du mois, 1957.

Histoire d'Allemagne. Hachette, 1965.

Histoire d'Angleterre. Fayard, n. d. (1937). Nouvelle édition, Michel, 1963.

Histoire de la France. Dominique Wapler, 1947.

Histoire des Etats-Unis, 1492–1946. Editions Albin Michel, 1947.

Histoire du peuple américain. Editions littéraires de France, n. d. (1955).

Hollande, présentation par André Maurois. "Les Albums des Guides Bleus." Hachette, 1955.

If Louis XVI Had Had an Atom of Firmness. London: Longmans, Green, 1931. French version in *Mes Songes que voici* under the title *Si Louis XVI.*

L'Instinct du bonheur. Grasset, 1934.

Introduction à la méthode de Paul Valéry. Editions des Cahiers libres, 1933. Incorporated into *Etudes littéraires.*

La Jeunesse devant notre temps. Flammarion, 1937.

Journal d'un tour en Amérique Latine. Les éditions du Bateau ivre, 1948.

Journal d'un tour en Suisse. Aux Portes de France, 1948.

Journal Etats-Unis 1946. Les Editions du Bateau ivre, 1946.

Lafayette in America. Boston: Houghton Mifflin, 1960.

Lecture mon doux plaisir. Fayard, n. d. (1957). Critical essays on French and foreign authors most of which had already appeared in other collections.

Lélia ou la vie de George Sand. Hachette, 1952.

Léon Tolstoi, le bonheur conjugal et "La Sonate à Kreutzer" avec une étude biographique inédite de André Maurois. Vial, 1953.

Lettres à l'inconnue. La Jeune Parque, 1953.

Londres. Grenoble: Arthaud, n. d. (1936).

Lord Byron et le démon de la tendresse. A l'enseigne de la porte étroite, 1925.

Louis XIV à Versailles. Hachette, 1955.

Lyautey. Plon, 1931.

La Machine à lire les pensées. Gallimard, 1937. Incorporated into *Les mondes impossibles.*

Magiciens et logiciens. Grasset, 1935.

Meïpe ou la Déliverance. Grasset, 1926. Incorporated into *Les Mondes imaginaires.*

Malte. Editions Alpina, 1935.

Mémoires. New York: Editions de la Maison française, 1942.

Mes Songes que voici, Essais et journaux de voyage. Grasset, 1933.

Mon ami Léger. Comment je conçois la figure. Carré, 1952.

La Monarchie anglaise de Victoria à Georges VI. Flammarion, 1937.

Le Monde de Marcel Proust. Hachette, 1960. Profusely illustrated. The text consists of pages excerpted from *A la recherche de Marcel Proust.*

Les Mondes imaginaires. Grasset, 1929. Includes *Meïpe, Les Souffrances du jeune Werther, Par la faute de M. de Balzac, Portrait d'une actrice.*

Les Mondes impossibles. Récits et nouvelles fantastiques. Editions de la Nouvelle Revue Française, 1947. Includes *Le Peseur des âmes, La Machine à lire les pensées, Voyage au pays des Articoles, Le Pays de trente-six mille volontés, Patapoufs et Filifers.*

Napoléon. Hachette, 1963.

Ni ange, ni bête. Grasset, 1919.

Nico, le petit garçon changé en chien. Calmann Lévy, 1955.

Les Nouveaux discours du docteur O'Grady. Grasset, 1950.

Olympio, ou la vie de Victor Hugo. Hachette, 1954.

Les Origines de la guerre de 1939. Gallimard, 1939.

Les Pages immortelles de Voltaire. Editions Corréa, n. d. (1938). Published in New York by Longmans, 1939, as *Living Thoughts of Voltaire.*

Paris. 128 photographies hors texte. Nathan, 1951.

Par la faute de M. de Balzac. Champion, 1923. Incorporated into *Les Mondes imaginaires.*

Patapoufs et Filifers. Hartmann, 1930. Incorporated into *Les Mondes impossibles.*

Le Pays de trente-six mille volontés. Les Editions des Portiques, 1928. Incorporated into *Les Mondes impossibles.*

Périgord. Présentation d' André Maurois. "Les Albums des Guides Bleus." Hachette, 1955.

Le Peseur d'âmes. Gallimard, 1931. Incorporated into *Les Mondes impossibles.*

Petite histoire de l'Espèce humaine. Les Cahiers de Paris, 1927.

Le Poème de Versailles. Grasset, n. d. (1954).

Portrait de la France et des Français. Hachette, 1955.

Portrait d'un ami qui s'appelait moi. Namur, Belgium: Wesmael-Charlier, 1959.

Portrait d'une actrice. Tremois, 1925. Incorporated into *Les Mondes imaginaires.*

Premiers contes. Rouen: Desfontaine, 1935.

Problèmes d'aujourd'hui. Larousse, 1952. In collaboration with Louis de Broglie, Albert Caquet, and Georges Duhamel.

Prométhée, la vie de Balzac. Hachette, 1964.

Proust et Ruskin. Oxford: University Press, 1932.

Public Libraries and Their Mission. Paris: Unesco, 1961.

Quatre études anglaises. L'Artisan du livre, 1927.

Relativisme. S. Kra, "Collection du XXe siècle," Vol. IV. Incorporated into *Mes Songes que voici.*

Retour en France. New York: Editions de la Maison française, 1947.

Selected Bibliography

Robert et Elizabeth Browning. Portraits, suivis de quelques autres. Grasset, 1955. An alternate title is *Portraits.*

Le Roman et le romancier. Monaco: Société des Conférences, Imprimérie de Monaco, 1929.

Les Roses de septembre. Flammarion, n. d. (1956).

Rouen. Emile-Paul, 1927. Incorporated into *Mémoires.*

Rouen dévasté. Rouen: Société normande des amis du livre, 1947.

Sentiments et coutumes. Grasset, 1934.

Sept visages de l'amour. Editions de la jeune Parque, 1946. Previously published with two less chapters as *Cinq visages de l'amour.*

Les Silences du colonel Bramble. Grasset. 1918.

Les Souffrances du jeune Werther. Jacques Schiffrin, Editions de la Pléiade, 1926. Incorporated into *Les Mondes imaginaires.*

Supplément à "Melanges et pastiches" de Marcel Proust. Editions du Trianon, 1928. Reprinted in 1932 by Gallimard under the title *Le Côté de Chelsea.*

Sur le vif. Lithographes de Degorce. Texte d'André Maurois. Libraire Eos, 1931.

Terre Promise. New York: Editions de la Maison française, 1945.

Toujours l'inattendu arrive. Editions des Deux-Rives, 1946.

Tourgeniev. Grasset, 1931.

Tragédie en France. New York: Editions de la Maison française, 1940.

Les Trois Dumas. Hachette, 1957.

Tu ne commettras pas d'adultère. Albin Michel, 1947.

Versailles aux lumières. Photographies d'Hélène Jeanbrau. Editions Tel, 1954.

Victor Hugo. Collection "Biographies par l'image," 1966.

La Vie de Disraeli. Gallimard, 1927.

La vie de Joseph Smith. Edouard Champion et ses amis, 1927.

La Vie de Sir Alexander Fleming. Hachette, 1959.

Voltaire. Gallimard, 1935.

Voyage au pays des Articoles. Jacques Schiffrin, Editions de la Pléiade, 1927. Incorporated into *Les Mondes impossibles.*

Washington, the Life of a Patriot. Didier, 1946.

Oeuvres complètes, 16 Vols. Grasset, 1950–1956.

Miscellaneous Works and Short Pieces first published in *Les Oeuvres libres.*

L'Amour en exil. #47 (1950).

Amour et tristesse du poète (Hugo). #94 (1954).

Cecil Rhodes. #86 (1953).

La Hausse et la baisse. #13 (1922). Incorporated into *Bernard Quesnay.*

Etats-Unis, 1948. #33 (1944).

Marcel Proust de 1906 à 1922. #30 (1949 Trois chapitres inédits de *A la recherche de Marcel Proust.*

Quand la France s'enrichissait. #21 (1947).

Le Roman de George Sand et de Chopin. #65 (1951).

Souvenirs d'enfance et de jeunesse. #17 (1947).

Translations from English by André Maurois

David Garnett, *La Femme changée en renard,* Trans. with the collaboration of Jane Simone Bussy. Grasset, 1924.

Elizabeth Barrett Browning, *Sonnets à la Portugaise.* Editions Brentano, 1946.

Laurence Housman, *Victoria Regina,* comédie en quatre actes et douze tableaux. Adaptation française d'André Maurois et Virginia Vernon. *L'Illustration,* 1937.

English Translations of Maurois' Major Works

Adrienne, la vie de la marquise de Lafayette
   Adrienne, the life of the Marquise

de Lafayette, trans. by Gerard Hopkins. New York: McGraw-Hill, 1961.

A la recherche de Marcel Proust
Proust, Portrait of a Genius, trans. by Gerard Hopkins. New York: Harper and Bros. 1950.

L'Anglaise et autres femmes
Ricochets, Miniature Tales of Human Life, trans. by Hamish Miles. New York: Harpers, 1935.

Ariel, ou la vie de Shelley
Ariel, the Life of Shelley, trans. by Ella D'Arcy. New York: Ungar, 1952.

Un Art de vivre
The Art of Living, trans. by James Whitall. New York: Harpers, 1958.

Aspects de la biographie
Aspects of Biography, trans. by S. C. Roberts. New York: Appleton, 1929.

Bernard Quesnay
Bernard Quesnay, trans. by Brian W. Downs. New York: Appleton, 1927.

Byron
Byron, trans. by Hamish Miles. New York: Appleton, 1930.

Cecil Rhodes
Cecil Rhodes, trans. by Rohan Wadham. London: Collins, 1953.

Cercle de famille
The Family Circle, trans. by Hamish Miles. New York: Appleton, 1932.

Chateaubriand
Chateaubriand, trans. by Vera Fraser, New York: Harpers, 1938.

Climats
Atmosphere of Love, trans. by Joseph Collins. New York: Appleton, 1929.

Le Côté de Chelsea
Chelsea Way, trans. by Hamish Miles, London: Mathews and Marrot, 1930.

Cours de bonheur conjugal
The Art of Being Happily Married, a Play, trans. by Crystal Herbert. New York: Harpers, 1953.

Destins exemplaires
Profiles of Great Men, trans. by Helen T. Patterson. Ipswich (England): Tower Bridge, 1954.

Les Deux géants
From the New Freedom to the New Frontier, trans. by Patrick O'Brien. New York: D. McKay, 1963.

Dialogues sur le commandement
Captains and Kings, trans. by J. L. May. New York: Appleton, 1925.

Les Discours du docteur O'Grady
The Return of Dr. O'Grady, trans. by Gerard Hopkins. London: Bodley Head, 1951.

Edouard VII et son temps
The Edwardian Era, trans. by Hamish Miles, New York: Appleton, 1935.

Un Essai sur Dickens
Dickens, trans. by Hamish Miles. New York: Harpers, 1935.

Histoire d'Angleterre
A History of England, trans. by Hamish Miles. London: Bodley Head, 1956.

Histoire de la France
A History of France, trans. by Henry L. Binsse and Gerard Hopkins. New York: Farrar, Straus and Cudahy, 1957.

Histoire des Etats-Unis
A New History of the United States, trans. by Denver and Jane Lindley, London: Lane, 1948.

L'Instinct du bonheur
A Time for Silence, trans. by Edith Johannsen. New York: Appleton, 1942.

Journal, Etats-Unis, 1946
From My Journal, trans. by Joan Charles. New York: Harpers, 1948.

Lélia, ou la vie de George Sand
Lelia, The Life of George Sand, trans. by Gerard Hopkins. New York: Harpers, 1953.

Lyautey
Lyautey, trans. by Hamish Miles. New York: Appleton, 1931.

La Machine à lire les pensées
The Thought-reading Machine, trans. by James Whitall. New York: Harpers, 1938.

Magiciens et logiciens
Prophets, and Poets, trans. by Hamish Miles. New York: Harpers, 1935.

Meïpe, ou la délivrance
Mape, trans. by Eric Sutton. New York: Appleton, 1926.

Mémoires
I Remember, I Remember, trans. by Denver and Jane Lindley. New York: Harpers, 1942.

Mes Songes que voici
A Private Universe, trans. by Hamish Miles. New York: Appleton, 1932.

Olympio ou la vie de Victor Hugo
Olympio, the Life of Victor Hugo, trans. by Gerard Hopkins. New York: Harpers, 1956.

Patapoufs et Filifers
Fatapoufs and Thinifers, trans. by Rosemary Benét. New York: Holt, 1940.

Le Pays de trente-six mille volontés
The Country of Thirty-Six Thousand Wishes, trans. by Pauline Fairbanks. New York: Appleton, 1930.

Le Peseur d'âmes
The Weigher of Souls, trans. by Hamish Miles. New York: Appleton, 1931.

Prométhée, la vie de Balzac
Prometheus, The Life of Balzac, trans. by Norman Denny. New York: Harper and Row, 1965.

Le Roses de septembre
September Roses, trans. by Gerard Hopkins. New York: Harpers, 1958.

Sept Visages d'amour
Seven Faces of Love, trans. by Haakon M. Chevalier. New York: Didier, 1944.

Les Silences du colonel Bramble
The Silence of Colonel Bramble, trans. by Thurfrida Wake. New York: Lane, 1920.

Terre promise
Woman without Love, trans. by Joan Charles. New York: Harpers, 1945.

Tragédie en France
Tragedy in France, trans. by Denver Lindley. New York: Harper, 1940.

Les Trois Dumas
The Titans, trans. by Gerard Hopkins. New York: Harpers, 1957.

La Vie de Disraeli
Disraeli, trans. by Hamish Miles. New York: Appleton, 1928.

La Vie de Sir Alexander Fleming
The Life of Sir Alexander Fleming, Discoverer of Penicillin, trans. by Gerard Hopkins. New York: Dutton, 1959.

Voltaire
Voltaire, trans. by Hamish Miles. New York: Appleton, 1932.

Voyage au pays des Articoles
A Voyage to the Island of the Articoles, trans. by David Garnett. New York: Appleton, 1929.

SECONDARY SOURCES

Books about Maurois

Droit, Michel, *André Maurois.* Editions universitaires, 1953. A fairly recent useful work on Maurois' overall achievements as a writer. Workmanlike and to the point.

Guéry, Suzanne, *La Pensée d'André Maurois.* Deux rives, 1941. An attempt to get at the philosophy of Maurois by examining his work. A helpful study.

Larg, David G., *André Maurois.* New York: Oxford University Press, 1942. A discursive essay written a long time ago that has little if any value left in it at this date.

Lemaître, Georges, *André Maurois.* Palo Alto: Stanford University Press, 1939. The best and most perceptive study of Maurois. The judgments expressed are still sound.

Sauvenier, Justin, *Mes amitiés spirituelles, André Maurois.* Brussels: Editions de Belgique, 1932. An early book, no longer very useful.

Suffel, Jacques, *André Maurois.* Flammarion, 1963. A tendentious work in which the writer uses his comments to elicit replies from the author. Its best feature is the alternation of remarks by Suffel and the comments or replies by Maurois. This work has all the advantages of an interview without the disadvantages of question and answer. For the student of Maurois it is invaluable.

Index

Index